INSIDE
THE GPO
1916

INSIDE THE GPO 1916

A FIRST-HAND ACCOUNT

INTRODUCTION BY ROBERT BALLAGH

EDITED BY MAURICE GOOD

JOE GOOD

THE O'BRIEN PRESS
DUBLIN

First published 2015 by The O'Brien Press Ltd,
12 Terenure Road East, Rathgar, Dublin 6, Ireland.
Tel: +353 1 4923333; Fax: +353 1 4922777
E-mail: books@obrien.ie; Website: www.obrien.ie
First published 1996 by Brandon.

ISBN: 978-1-84717-718-6

All quotations, in English and Irish, have been reproduced with original spelling and punctuation.

Printed and bound by CPI Group (UK) Ltd, Croydon, CR0 4YY
The paper used in this book is produced using pulp from managed forests.

PICTURE CREDITS

The author and publisher wish to thank the following for permission to use photographs
and illustrative material: the Good family: section 1, p.1, p.6. National Library of Ireland:
section 1, p.4 (bottom left and right), p.5 (top). Honor Ó Brolcháin: section 1, p.3 (top).
Lorcan Collins: section 1, p.2 (both), p.4 (top right), p.7 (top); section 2, p.1 (top), pp. 2–3,
p.4 (both), p.5, p.6. Kilmainham Gaol Museum: section 1, p.3 (bottom), p.4 (top left), p.5
(bottom), p.7 (bottom), p.8 (both); section 2, p.1 (bottom), p.7, p.8 (both).

ACKNOWLEDGEMENTS

I want to thank my sister Joan, my brothers Kevin and John, my son
Stephen Good and Una O'Neill; Susan Malley, Dr Aidan Clarke and
his wife Mary; and all at Brandon. My thanks are also due to Michael
Kenny, Curator at the National Museum of Ireland and of the 1916–22
Exhibit, Kildare Street, Dublin; the librarians at the Westminster
Libraries in London, the Rathmines Public Libraries, and others at the
National Newspaper Archives, Hendon, and the Public Records Office,
Kew; to Nora Kennedy and Corinna Bickford, Ted Doyle, Kevin Good
Jr and his wife Aileen, Jacinta Conaty, Ian Skeffington, Joe Caswall,
Ann and Richard Munn, Phyllis Ryan, Dr James Greenlee, Dr Kathryn
Bindon and the Theatre Department at the Memorial University in
Newfoundland.

Maurice Good

Dublin, August 1996

CONTENTS

INTRODUCTION

The key significance of this stirring account of the Easter Rising and the War of Independence is that it is told not by a professional writer or historian, but by someone who was there; someone who actually experienced, at first hand, those seminal events in Irish history. This is what invests the narrative with such freshness and integrity.

The book's author, Joe Good, was born in Soho, London, in 1895. He quickly developed an interest in his Irish background. As a young man, he enrolled in the Irish Volunteers – the same night as Michael Collins. In 1916 they, together with many English-born men, travelled to Dublin to participate in the Easter Rising. Until I read Joe Good's account, I was unaware of just how many Londoners were in the GPO during Easter week. In our chequered history, it's amazing to record how often our exiles have answered Ireland's call!

INSIDE THE GPO

Joe Good was a modest man. His version of those tumultuous years is not a vainglorious one, simply a setting-out of the facts as he saw them. In the course of the narrative, he provides us with a personal and honest portrayal of the leaders; this in turn gives us a unique insight into the motivations behind the Rising.

As the centenary of the Easter Rising approaches, Joe Good's vivid account is a timely reminder of our responsibility to ensure that the bravery and sacrifice of an exceptional generation of Irish men and women are adequately commemorated. Yet, as we prepare to salute their unprecedented courage in taking on the might of the British Empire, we must not lose sight of the reasons why they embarked on such a daring challenge in the first place.

In my opinion, the men and women of 1916 were not merely rebels, but people of vision. What they desired was not simply a government in Dublin, a green flag over Dublin Castle and a harp on the coinage – they were calling for a cultural revolution, for a transformation of both public and personal reality. The outline of that transformation is contained in a truly remarkable document, the Proclamation of the Republic. It pledged the right of the people of Ireland to the ownership of Ireland and to the unfettered control of Irish destinies; the right to national freedom and sovereignty; the right to religious and civil liberty, equal rights and equal opportunities for all Irish citizens; and the right to the pursuit of the happiness and prosperity of the whole nation and all its parts, cherishing all the children of the nation equally. Those inspiring ideals were ratified when the first Dáil met in 1919, and later defended in the War of Independence.

I believe we should take advantage of the focus created by the anniversaries to examine the Ireland of today, and to question whether the dreams and aspirations of a truly heroic generation have been fulfilled. For instance: who owns Ireland today, its natural resources, its mineral wealth? Do we, as Irish citizens, have unfettered control of our destinies? Can we say we are a fully free and sovereign nation today? Tragically, the honest answer to all those fundamental questions is a resounding 'No'!

However, instead of dwelling on the failures of today's generation, I believe we would be far better served by looking ahead. We should draw inspiration from the courage and vision of Joe Good and his comrades, and initiate a nationwide dialogue on the shape of a new Ireland that would serve the interests of all its citizens. Such a democratic and visionary project would represent a far more fitting tribute to a heroic generation than the erection of a ceremonial viewing stand, packed with so-called dignitaries, outside the GPO on Easter Sunday, 2016.

Robert Ballagh, Dublin, 2015

PREFACE

THIS IS MY father's journal, his account of the events he witnessed when he fought in the 1916 Easter Rising and the War of Independence that followed. It is a personal testimony, a story of rebellion written by a man of fifty-one about his actions as a young revolutionary.

In 1946, thirty years after the events of Easter Week, he finally yielded to my demands to write of his experience. The journal that resulted was written on 2s 6d copybooks, in my father's clear and even hand. At this time, too, Joe gave evidence to an official commission that interviewed veterans of the Rising, and he later received a transcript of his testimony. This journal became a composite blend of both sources. I have edited the text, occasionally expanding a familial 'shorthand' that would confuse the general reader, though the rest of Joe's writing remains unaltered.

INSIDE THE GPO

My father never imagined that his words would be published. He was a modest man, who loved talk when it was other people's, but was himself happy to watch and listen. He never spoke of his own glory, nor of his small place in Irish history, any more than my mother, Mary Ellen Donovan, would speak of her family connections with renowned Fenians – of O'Donovan Rossa, or of Richard O'Sullivan Burke, her great-uncle who fought in the uprising of 1867 and with Garibaldi's Italian Risorgimento. My father shared her reticence and extreme distaste for 'heroics', and made no show of his worth, though others did.

Joe Good was born in Soho in 1895. Despite his English patronymic and the fact that his mother's surname was Spencer, he believed he came from Irish stock. He was christened Alfred Joseph, but shortened that name to Joe, de-Anglicising it as part of his changing identity when he became involved in the nascent Irish revolutionary movement in Edwardian London. He enrolled in the Irish Volunteers, in the same group as Michael Collins, and from the outbreak of the First World War campaigned against Kitchener and Redmond's recruitment of Irishmen for the Flemish abattoirs.

He left for Dublin in 1916, one of many English-born men who would rather serve the Republic. This he did in Easter Week and through the War of Independence, when he worked closely with Michael Collins, for whom he had a special respect and affection. After the Treaty and Britain's withdrawal from the Twenty-six Counties, he resigned his commission in the Free State army rather than participate in the fratricidal Civil War that broke out in 1922. But the death of Michael Collins early in that conflict was for Joe a personal trauma, an event from which he could not walk away. He rejoined the army immediately after Collins' funeral, and served until the end of the Civil War; then, having completed this duty, he returned to civilian life.

For much of that life, my father worked as the maintenance-electrician in the College of Science, Dublin (now restored in much magnificence as Government House), and raised four children with his wife Mary Ellen. He loved his family, his friends and his books. He was an avid reader, and later in his life he wrote a number of prose pieces – studies rather than stories, as he had little time or taste for fiction.

This journal, however, is his earliest work. It reflects well the man who wrote it: it is clear-headed, wry and always honest. Joe remained throughout a detached and ironic observer of the doomed rebellion. He witnessed with a distinctly English incredulity the absurdity of the rebels' heroism; he never forgot the sight of his aristocratic commanding officer, the poet Joseph Mary Plunkett, reading Erasmus' In Praise of Folly as shells exploded around them in the GPO and Joyce's Seventh City of Christendom went up in flames. This memoir was written by a streetwise Cockney youth who distrusted heroics, though he could respond to the valour of his leaders and comrades.

Late in his life, when I asked him to send me this manuscript so that I might consult it for a play I was writing, he added a comment at the top of the first page: 'I don't think it's of any great value – I've grown up a little in my acquaintance with good writing since I wrote this.' I've grown up more than a little myself while editing these extraordinary pages. It's not often that one can resume a relationship with one's father in such a way. Here he is then, equipped with his phenomenal memory, his exceptional eye, and his ear cocked so closely to history.

Hamlet:	My father. Methinks I see my father.
Horatio:	O! Where, my lord?
Hamlet:	In my mind's eye, Horatio.

Maurice Good, Dublin, 1996

London Years

PERHAPS THIS NARRATIVE is hardly worth the two and sixpence spent on the paper; and even then may not be completed. I am dilatory, and have had thirty years during which I might have written it, when the personalities and incidents were fresher in my mind. As to precise dates, I have no intention of checking; any historical references can be confirmed from competent writers on the period. As to the facts, they are as I honestly believe them to be, and in speaking of any personalities I have tried to be without bias.

You have asked for it[1] – this narrative – and I consented to write it mainly so that I might see the why and the wherefore of all the effervescence that contributed so largely to the success of the 1916 Rising. Incidentally, the bubbling has not yet subsided.

---

1 There is an inscription 'To Maurice, Aged 13, 1946' before the opening paragraph in the first book of manuscript.

Make no mistake about it, the emotional depths to which the people of Ireland were stirred were the main cause of the revolution's success. Yet for the life of me I cannot understand how a logical people – who often shot the landlords as a remedy for Irish national grievances, as well as to get possession of the peasant holdings – thought that they could, and did, end British rule in four-fifths of Ireland mainly by flags, banners, meetings and hysteria.

For at no time during the period from 1916 to the truce in 1921 were there more than 2,000 rifles in the hands of the Irish Volunteers or what was, later, called the IRA. Indeed, as late as August 1920, there were not more than ten rifles in the Mid-Limerick Brigade, Limerick being one of the most active areas of confrontation with the British. It would be interesting to assess how many rifles there were in Ireland after the Rising of 1916. They were terribly few. Most of the weapons were captured after the Rising and could never be replaced. The 2,000 I mention I believe to be an exaggeration.

But whilst the Irish could not have put two battalions in the field, they fought and defeated the British armed and unarmed forces: for certainly the British did not withdraw because they wanted to.

On the face of it, the Irish achieved what appeared to be quite impossible: such a small body defeated an army of 20,000 troops, about 5,000 armed police and a favoured and powerful section of the community who had most of the privileges and possessions from the time of Cromwell. Then how was it done?

In the last resort, when all the heroic posturings were of no avail, there grew out of our movement a very small branch called the ASU – the Active Service Unit. This unit was made up of men drawn mainly from Dublin and London. The question was seriously debated at Volunteer HQ – *why* previous risings had failed? It was agreed that there were three main factors: intemperance, talking and informers.

The hardcore Irish Republican Brotherhood (a secret society condemned by the Catholic Church) – the activists who fuelled the rebellion in 1916 and the resistance movement that followed – unofficially appointed their own officers. The IRB was a watertight elite, and the Volunteers (long before 1916) were either abnormally sober, or never drank. So informers could be identified and liquidated by an efficient intelligence system. Better still, those who sought and paid for information – the RIC (Royal Irish Constabulary) and other British civil servants – could be killed or terrified. They were the eyes and ears of the British administration. Our ASU were armed mostly with revolvers. Their job was mainly to execute on orders British agents or those who supplied them with information at any time and place, to put out the eyes of the British administration in Ireland. By August 1920[2], the eyes of the enemy *were* put out.

Most of the actions in the country against the British after 1916 were spontaneous, without direction from our GHQ. When winter was coming in 1920 and I knew the British would hit back, I asked a member of our GHQ what were their plans, if any, for our campaign. His reply was, 'Ah – we are still only discussing the next stunt!'

'This happy few, this band of killers' – that was the name it went by in Dublin – put the fear of God into the British administration in Ireland, and no doubt into quite a few Irish politicians. It dawned on the British, I imagine, that whilst assassination could be met with assassination, that for every assassin *they* made, we in Ireland could produce two; that the game was up, and that suppressing the national revolution would mean a reconquest of Ireland, and God knew how many hangings that might involve. When would reconquest pay a dividend? The British did not know the strength of the force they were fighting, and the Irish leaders had not the faintest idea how or when or if the end would come. They lived from day to day, and sufficient to the day was the ambush thereof. Historians no doubt will try to show the period of 1916 to 1921 as a period when there was a definite insurgent army and nation with campaigns and battles. It will be a damned lie.

---

2 The ASU of the Dublin Brigade and the 'Squad' of the intelligence section wiped out much of British intelligence in Dublin on 21 November 1920, 'Bloody Sunday'.

The insurrection of 1916 was a blossoming of seeds sown in the past by unimaginative rulers. The aftermath of 1916 and the reaction to the execution of the leaders was the natural reaction of a people who have strong personal ties with each other, and react as members of a family when an injury is done to one of them – without regard to the original cause. Had any member of our movement been asked this question: 'Do you expect to drive British administration bag and baggage out of the greater part of Ireland?' – he could not truthfully have said 'yes'.

One of the main reasons for the activities after 1916 was the clannish temperament of Irishmen. Dublin had, so to speak, justified its existence. Corkmen and southern Irishmen had not had the opportunity to put up so good a show, because their mobilisation was countermanded. They were resentful and angry, and were longing for an opportunity to have a crack at the British. The first action occurred in Cork and Tipperary. The Volunteer headquarters in Dublin again and again tried to restrain this. It was a case of the tail wagging the dog; most likely the fact that Collins was a County Cork man made it possible for him to guide, restrain, and give them final absolution.

What happened in early 1920 in southern Ireland, including the audacious attacks on the RIC and their barracks, was received with amazement in Dublin. 'Little Apples' had grown again, but they were not the fruit expected by those who had made that epic stand in 1916. The Dublin Volunteers, on the whole, were content with their past laurels. Perhaps understandably so.

Much ink and some blood has been spilt for and against the Treaty which was signed in London by Arthur Griffith and Collins. It was said and believed by many, in all sincerity, that another round should be fought. But for those of us who had brought into being the Terrible Beauty – to use Yeats' words – there was but one obvious end to the revolution: to be hanged by the neck, because by 1921 our Active Service Unit, and a few daring spirits, had all but reached the end of their tether. So far as I know, no biographer or historian has asked this question: what had Collins left of real fighting material? And what responsibility had he for those he had brought to the shadow of the scaffold? If he was a soldier – and he was always that – his first duty was to his subordinates and comrades.

In conclusion, then: in five years, from 1916 to 1921, the freedom of the greater part of Ireland was achieved. It is now 1946, and so far as I see, there has not been in all these years any realistic effort to secure complete autonomy. Nor, as far as I am aware, has there been any plan for doing so. Will 'little apples' grow again, and a few romantic realists sweep all those who sleep on their laurels into oblivion? The apparent contradiction of 'romantic realists' is an appropriate one for such paradoxical zealots.

EARLY YEARS – 'THE GAEL IS GONE'

When I was a small boy in London, it was said during a speech in the British House of Commons: 'The Gael is gone, gone with a vengeance.' And this was said long after those terrible famines of 1847 to 1867. That remark stuck and still sticks in my mind – 'great is the potency of the spoken word'. The description of the insurrection of 1798 made quite an impression on me as a boy in a London-Irish family, where I heard many speak of those poor pitiable peasant pikemen, and how their distended stomachs, filled with raw grain, had in death burst so that their entrails entangled the wheels of the wagons on which they were taken for burial. Poor 'Croppies'. I felt something should be done about it someday. I was not then familiar with Pope's *Iliad,* in which Hector's 'entrails streamed along the ground'!

But in due course I was to see the bright pink lungs of one Irishman, exposed by a fellow Irishman, strewn on a newly tarred road, and reflect on Pope's cheerful lines. Truly, no one should have anything to do with revolution unless he possesses a strong stomach.

I was about fifteen when I first read a little of Irish history. I was rather a solitary and very imaginative young fellow, and kept my real musing to myself. I had read a good many of Walter Scott's novels, and was impressed by Ivanhoe. I had plenty of time to daydream. From the age of fourteen to sixteen-and-a-half, I worked in a weaving and spinning factory. My job was to keep the wheel turning for the spinner – not a very arduous task. I turned the spinning wheel for the foreman; this I could do with one hand and, by putting my book on a shelf, could read at the same time. I read anything I could get, even girls' 'yellow-back' novels, to avoid the monotony of turning a wheel from half-eight each morning to seven-thirty at night. I was going soft in the brain from monotony and reading tripe – and knew it.

'Let me write the ballads of a people –
I care not who makes their laws ...'[3]

A rare and refreshing element suddenly arrived. My sister Agnes had joined an Irish political society and also attended the branch of the newly founded Gaelic League in London. She brought home old Irish songs and ballads – those of James Clarence Mangan and Thomas Davis – and Thomas Moore's poems and melodies were heard by me for the first time: 'The Erne shall run red with redundance of blood'; 'When boyhood's fire was in my veins'; 'To strike a blow for you, dear land'; 'When he who adores thee'; 'She is far from the land where her young hero sleeps.'

---

3 Andrew Fletcher of Saltoun (1704): 'If a man were permitted to make all the ballads, he need not care who should make the laws of a nation.' I prefer Joe's version.

These were thoughts that had run in my head since child-hood, and that I had never heard expressed – till now. I lapped them up without effort, and memorised hundreds of songs and ballads. I once bet Mick[4] Collins that I knew more Irish songs, ballads and poems than he – during the time we were in Frongoch Prison Camp together after the 1916 Rising. I remembered about two hundred and fifty, he about one hundred more than I. But then he always had a phenomenal memory.

Perhaps the desire for action among those of Irish blood in London and elsewhere in England was caused by the old Irish Parliamentary Party in the House of Commons. God how those Irish MPs talked! Their speeches were reported verbatim in the Sunday papers, and were read out in their entirety in most working-class Irish households. How I hated to hear the phrases that in the reports interrupted long meandering speeches: 'Loud Cheers'; 'Laughter'; 'Loud Laughter!' Many a Sunday at home, I listened to those speeches being read aloud and longed to hear that one of the 'Right Honourable Gentlemen' had thrown something or spat in someone's eye, but it never happened. The speeches went on and on and on, and our parents looked forward to more of it.

There was a colony of Irish Catholics in every English city, the sons and daughters of those who were driven out

---

4 Throughout the journal, my father usually writes 'Mick' Collins, as he also always did in speaking of him at home and amongst old comrades or friends.

of Ireland by the famine and Irish landlordism. They had remained Catholics in the main, and had a sentimental regard for Robert Emmett and – of all people – Gladstone, that one-time champion of Home Rule for Ireland. They were to beget sons who would take the Post Office in Dublin, garrison it for a week's stand, and be commemorated there later in a bronze statue of that legendary warrior-hero of Irish epic – Cú Chulainn.

THE GAELIC LEAGUE IN LONDON

'He who cannot with his tongue win a "Nation" is no man ...' to misquote Byron, I think, who won many a woman. When my sister, Agnes, joined the Gaelic League, it was with some misgivings, I imagine, that she took me to my first Gaelic class. My appearance was nothing to speak of; one could not do a lot sartorially on two and nine pence per week pocket money and clothing allowance. So I took no part in the Irish class, and sat on a school-desk and waited beside a some-what delicate and intelligent looking boy to witness the Irish 'folk-dancing'. I never knew his name, but he gave me one of the shocks of my life.

He was reading a small two-paged paper, about ten inches square, and in due course passed it to me. Herein, frankly stated, was the argument of 'direct action' and 'physical force'; the printed words were, as I have said, in my mind for many years, and now someone had published them. This Gaelic League journal was named *An Claidheamh Soluis*. I was told much later that 'Solus' meant light, and 'Claidheamh' was the word for sword in Gaelic; but on that instant that paper was a sword of light to me!

The Gaelic Leaguers were quite a new experience for me; they were mainly civil servants and schoolteachers, a step up the social ladder from my usual associates. Still, if you would try to learn Irish, they would accept you like a brother. Gaelic was not my dish – I was no student – but I thought then as I watched them that their gospel would endure, and was beyond corruption, and would outlive physical violence.

Strange as it may seem, the Gaelic League held many of its classes in British Protestant schools. Even then, John Bull was very tolerant in his own house. And that was all I got out of the Gaelic League – that small paper every now and again from my new friend. It was plenty to satisfy. I used to carry it in my pocket, feeling somewhat like a small Guy Fawkes.

THE GAELIC ATHLETIC ASSOCIATION

The Gaelic Athletic Association occasionally held their sports at Herne Hill in London, and it was there I had my first sight of Mick Collins.

Mick was running a race and was finishing neck and neck with Joe Reilly; at one moment Joe would be in front, and then Mick. Suddenly Mick put on a spurt and, as he passed Joe, deliberately dug his elbow into the soft part of Joe's bent arm. The race finished; Joe was second, but there was no doubt who had fairly won the race. It struck me that day that Mick was the epitome of the individual who must win – at that period a more English than an Irish characteristic, which he'd acquired, maybe, working in the British civil service. This basic competitiveness was to fuel his talents later in beating the English at their own game. What Mick had done in that race was unpremeditated, but still as plain as a pikestaff – so much so that many people were laughing. Meanwhile, Joe and Mick were face to face, shouting at each other with that Clonakilty mellowness, that County Cork accent which is so mellifluous, even when belligerent.

I had gone to the sports that day in uniform. I was a member of a kind of military cadet organisation, the 'Catholic Boys' Brigade': the English Catholics must have had plenty of money, for it was a uniform similar to that worn by the Irish Guards. It must have been quite shocking to some of the Gaelic Leaguers and Gaelic Athletic Associates. Nothing was said to me, however, and I was unconscious of how out of place a British uniform was. Though I would not have left if asked to go, and would have explained why I was so dressed, by saying that 'If one would carry arms, one should learn the *use* of arms!' This, incidentally, was before the Irish Volunteers were formed in London. But, meanwhile, we

'Boys of the Catholic Brigade' were equipped with a small cavalry carbine, and were trained in foot-drill and bayonet exercises. I'm sure Mick noticed me that day; he always had vision, and would have recognised the significance of a military-type uniform.

He would have enjoyed the story of how I *left* the brigade. It came about this way. The brigade was giving a concert in George's Hall, London, and I was seated at the back of the stage. The Catholic cardinal appeared. The brigade stood to attention, and 'Faith of Our Fathers' was sung. This was followed by 'God Save the King'. I sat down. Fortunately, I was not in the front row. I was pulled to my feet. I promptly threw my hat down – a most insulting thing to do. I was thrown out of a side door, without my hat. I walked home bare-headed – but I had the carbine.

THE IRISH VOLUNTEERS

The first I heard of the Irish Volunteers in London was that a meeting would be held in the German gymnasium near King's Cross. I attended there, and was enrolled in the same group as Mick Collins[5]. One week later, he was in charge of the section. Mick promptly choked me off for the way I marched to attention – he had not yet learnt the necessity of the word 'halt', and I continued marching to attention until I

---

5 Michael Collins was enrolled 25 April 1914.

got that order. But in any case, I was too well trained to argue with an NCO – so I answered not at all.

A large number of young Irishmen in London joined the Irish Volunteers, about 2,000 in all; native-born Irishmen, they actually practised trench–digging in one of their sports fields. Many, on Redmond's parliamentary urging and the later Volunteer 'split'[6], had rushed like sheep to the trenches. But, in spite of the war and the split and economic pressures, there now remained only about a hundred men who were still available for the 1916 Rising in Dublin. Of this hundred, most were not born in Ireland at all, and, by a stroke of irony, were to take and garrison the General Post Office during the Easter Week insurrection. These expatriate 'Gaels' had returned with a vengeance!

The 1914 war had started. Home Rule for Ireland was now shelved for the duration – 'put on the statute book'. Newspaper headlines asserted that little 'Catholic Belgium' was being 'burned, raped and looted' – nuns were being 'murdered'; and thousands of young London-Irishmen and native Englishmen were rushed to be buried in the mud of Flanders.

On the declaration of war, many Germans marched out of London – thousands of them, waiters rolling up their aprons and marching to the railway stations in orderly columns.

---

6 On 20 September 1914, into Redmondite 'National Volunteers' and IRB-backed 'Irish Volunteers'.

I fell in with them once or twice, and spoke to those nearest to me, advising them to turn back and not be slaughtered for imperialism. I saw nothing illogical in what I hoped to do myself – which was to fight too, but fight for what was as remote as the stars.

From 1914 to 1916, I was employed as an assistant electrician. I'd given up my job as a wheelboy at sixteen-and-a-half, and got a job at seven shillings per week in a motor-car garage and workshop.

The automobile industry was in its infancy, so I got some knowledge, increased prestige – to my mind – but reduced myself, of necessity, to sixpence a week pocket money. I had to give up six and six at home. There was little income coming into the family. My father was dead, and there were three younger children.

After about three months, I was fired from the automobile industry; it was more economical to employ a youth who could pay a fee for an apprenticeship. (I had bucked at an alternative of being a messenger boy.) I was at a loose end, and prepared to take any blind-alley occupation, provided I got higher wages, fed up as I was after my sacrifice for a more ambitious future. But one could get eighteen shillings a week in London as a 'tricycle boy', more than twice my previous wages, and this job had the further lure of the open air! I took a tricycle job, and led the life of great dissipation for a while. The greater part of my work was canvassing for orders for tyres; I spent most of the sunny days at Hendon on the broad of my back, watching the flying planes. On a wet day, I spent my time in a coffee-house with a novel. The name of the firm I worked for was painted on the side of my box carrier, so I plastered a newspaper over this. It is amazing how far one can push a tricycle when young. I saw a good deal of the English countryside (ambition be hanged). I was enjoying myself when my joy was dispelled by an old schoolmate. He was shocked by what I had come to. I had earlier taught him to read. He told me he was working at steam-fitting, and he said that if I told a story convincingly, I could get a job in his firm as a fitter's mate, at about five pence an hour. So I told the story, got a job and was working at steam-fitting for about two years when the war broke out.

All wars present opportunities to the enterprising. Work in the building trade is intermittent. In August 1914, I was at the labour exchange and looking for a job. There was a sudden demand for fitters and electricians. I had handed in my card as a fitter's mate when I heard one of the clerks say, 'Is there an electrician's helper here?'

'Yes!' said I – whereupon he gave me a card of introduction to an electrical contractor. By this time, he had got possession of my unemployment card, on which I appeared as a fitter's mate. 'Hi,' said he, 'you are a fitter's mate!'

'You've made a mistake,' said I, and ran out of the exchange with the letter in my hand.

I had wanted to be an electrical engineer since I was very young. Opportunity had knocked at my door, and I knew that with the war on, I had my best chance. The engineer who interviewed me saw through my bluff. So I remarked that I was relatively intelligent, and that the business did not call for geniuses, judging by some of the electricians I'd seen. He laughed at my impudence and said, 'I have sent sixty men today to this job; fifty have returned – the conditions are tough – but at least by the look of you, you won't come back! I'll send you your ticket to Wiltshire and a postal order by tomorrow morning.'

He was as good as his word – there are some great people in this old world – and that's how I became an electrician. Of course, if one has an acquaintance with mechanics, and had already acquired some experience, it helps a lot.

I lived for twelve months in Salisbury, and saw little or nothing of the Irish Volunteers. The following year I spent working in London. I gave little attention to the technical side of my job; I was much more interested in Irish national-ist activities. *Nationality*, and other as transitory journals, were read avidly. The Volunteers, alas, had become very few. Every now and again, some of them would join the British army. But there was one place near Westminster where the Volun-teers met until the end of 1915. Here I often saw Eamon Tierney – and even then he was armed. I went away on a short country job in January 1916, and when I came back went to our drill hall, which, incidentally, was in a school. I learned that the few Volunteers who still existed were gone, or were shortly going ... to Dublin.

The sands were running out. The Conscription Bill was passed in England. There was now a register of men of military age, and I had not complied with that law. Redmond's voice, as an Irish parliamentary leader, was being drowned out in the advance of war. I felt he was a broken reed, and that the Irish Parliamentary Party would only make a whingeing protest when conscription was applied to Ireland. Soldiers, in my home, were referred to as the scrapings of hell. My father had been pro-Boer during the last British war. I had learned to hate and despise British imperialism. Incidentally, at that time British rule was more temperate than it had ever been in Ireland. But I knew no one in Ireland. I wrote to my father's relations, but they did not reply.

I had five pounds in my pocket, and boundless faith that I would never want for a meal in Ireland. So I took a return to Dublin for fifty shillings – a return ticket so that it would appear that I intended to return to England. I never shall return, for the British are not my people and their gods are not my gods.

DUBLIN

I ARRIVED IN DUBLIN on a bright February morning. Dun Laoghaire, Killiney and the Dublin mountains looked like a magic land. I had been on a steamship for the first time, and had only seen the seaside once and briefly. London was dull and grey and dismal in its blackout, a perpetual English Sunday, only lacking those depressing bells that summon the dead to service, for the living heed them not. The land approaching was my land of dreams, where I believed the impossible could be conceived and could then became a fact.

The North Wall station was a terrible let-down after the beautiful bay. One had the impression, on sighting Dublin from the sea, that beautiful green fields ran down to the sea. Instead of which, on leaving the boat, one went through a dark corridor into a depressing station, leading to a deserted street. It was early on Sunday morning, but in the station and in the streets outside there were armed sentries with fixed bayonets. This seemed threatening.

It is hard now to remember my first impressions of Dublin, but one thing stands out – the smell of the sea everywhere. And the rakish-looking electric trams without a roof – the driver exposed to the elements. They rattled a good deal on the cobbled roads, even in O'Connell Street (then called Sackville Street).

I got away quickly from the station. There were many people abroad, and when I went to the Pro-Cathedral for mass, I was struck by the crowds of well dressed, fresh-complexioned young men. I did not know till later that this was the 'grocers-curates'-mass, and that the men were young countrymen from all over Ireland.

I went into a modest hotel, Neary's of Parnell Square, which was near the tobacco shop of Tom Clarke, though I knew nothing at all of Tom – at that time – or, indeed, of the IRB.

As I already had affiliations with the Irish American Alliance, I told the young waitress at Neary's I wanted to contact a person in the 'Hibernian Rifles'[7]. I was very naive, and felt she was in sympathy with the Irish Volunteers – or should be.

One person I had been in contact with was Fergus O'Connor, the son I think of someone of that name well-

---

7 Like Dublin's Citizen Army, founded by Jim Larkin and James Connolly in 1913 after the great general strike and lock-out to protect the workers, the 'Hibernian Rifles' was yet another of the small revolutionary 'armies' of the time.

known in Irish history[8]. He was a member of the Irish American Alliance, a rival to Joe Devlin's Ancient Order of Hibernians. Fergus O'Connor was an Irish gentleman, courteous, well informed and very open-hearted. Indeed I believe his generosity eventually impoverished him. It was my good fortune to meet him and be his guest for a week or two. I was anxious to pay my way, having fifty shillings in hand, so he consented to let me pay his housekeeper one pound per week. He sold the half of my return ticket for a pound. This made it possible for me to pay my way for a while, and enabled me to leave his home later with my pride intact, having given a little gift to his manservant.

He did not know why I left. He probably thought I was well furnished with money; otherwise he would not have let me leave. But I was determined not to sponge on him, so I took myself back to my modest hotel near Clarke's shop. Believe it or not, in 1916, one could stay at that hotel, Neary's, for one pound a week, with three excellent meals a day and fine accommodations.

The first guest I met there was my friend, Johnny O'Connor, 'Blimey' as he became known amongst the Volunteers because of his Cockney accent. He had, like myself, just left London, to avoid conscription and to fight for another and better cause[9].

---

8 Presumably the Chartist leader and founder of *The Northern Star.*

9 Johnny O'Connor was a fellow Londoner – they both joined the Volunteers in London – and Joe's lifelong friend, even though they fought on opposite sides in the Civil War.

INSIDE THE GPO

We were not long in Neary's Hotel when things began
to happen. Gilbert Lynch, the trade union organiser, had
deposited a case containing arms and ammunition under his
bed, and in his absence the police had raided the hotel and
captured his stuff. Mick Collins very soon appeared on the
scene, looking for Lynch, and asked me 'What the ... hell' I
was doing 'in such an obvious place'. He told me to proceed to Larkfield in Kimmage. I did not dispute his orders,
although I did not know by what authority he gave them.

I was glad to go, however. The hotel was too hot to hold
us in any case, and I did not know if I could pay any more
hotel bills. Mick also ordered me to accompany Lynch to
Batt O'Connor's, where he was to be quartered. This I did –
though there wasn't much left of the cache of 'war-materials'
that Lynch had just brought over from Manchester.

THE KIMMAGE GARRISON

Count Plunkett (count of the Holy Roman Empire) and
his family resided on a small estate called Larkfield, at Kimmage. On the grounds of this small estate was a derelict flour
mill, a portion of which was used as a drill hall and shooting range for the 4th Battalion of the Dublin Brigade of the
Volunteers. The mill had been taken over by the Liverpool
Volunteers, and turned into a barracks. Sometime previous
to their arrival in Dublin, they had subscribed to a fund for

the purpose of maintaining themselves in Ireland, the mill being handed over to them by the Plunketts.

In due course, other Volunteers came over from England and, on arrival at Larkfield, became the guests of the Liverpool contingent. Some arrangement was come to, for the Liverpool funds must have been exhausted. Who put up the money I never bothered to find out; probably the Plunkett family. And there, when we reached our fullest strength, about ninety of us were quartered from February to Easter of 1916. Our numbers continued to swell, with men from Manchester, London, Liverpool and Glasgow, the majority of whom were born in England, though by far the greatest number came from Liverpool.

George Plunkett, who was in charge of us, shared our sleeping quarters in this draughty, obsolete mill. His bed, like ours, was a bag of straw on the hard boards. George was our 'Skipper', and ranked as captain. He was always in the uniform of the Volunteers while in barracks. He was a gentle soul, and it seemed inappropriate for him to be in charge of a pretty hard crowd.

We were referred to ironically as 'George's lambs' by the Plunkett family. Perhaps they named us well, for he led us to the slaughter – the greater part by far of George's lambs are dead.

The mill was an excellent training place for men likely to go into battle. The food was simple, wholesome and plentiful; the breezes blowing through the mill made us hardy and hungry. George kept us busy, taking us nightly on route marches. In the daytime, some of us were engaged in making crude pikes; others in filling shotgun cartridges with heavy shot, as large as peas.

Some of us were busiest for most of the time making crude hand-grenades out of 2" x 4" cast-iron down-pipe, with a flange-end through which a long bolt passed. A small hole penetrated one of the flanges, through which the fuse was inserted. The fuse was of sulphur or match type – that is to say, one struck it on some abrasive material before it was primed to throw. It was estimated to be a three-second bomb. It's doubtful if many of us were able to find out in advance how well they worked – though on one occasion, later, I almost did.

There were only two crude brass moulds for the shot-gun pellets, which turned out ten lead pellets per mould. One man held the pellet mould, and another poured the liquid lead. The brass expanded and became so hot that one handled the moulds with gloves or, alternatively, plunged them into a bucket of cold water. And our pellets were apt to have a ragged fringe of lead; these fringes we carefully trimmed off, lest it should be said that we fired 'dum-dum'.

On a night of a peak load – we worked day and night shifts – our output would be 5,000 lead pellets. The output of hand-grenades, when we had enough material, would be twenty an hour. The lead from which pellets were made was bought in scrapyards. Three, four or five shillings-worth was bought at a time, and was wheeled through the streets in hand-barrows. Sometimes, small parcels of lead would be handed to us by Volunteers of another battalion. The ammunition was distributed to Volunteer units as it was produced, so I'm not able to give an estimate of the total amount that was produced. But it was an impressive quantity.

There were occasional alarms. We mounted guard night and day, and we did not know when the British might come and dig us out. Obviously our immunity could not last. Meanwhile, we had a good deal of fun, a lovely view of the Dublin Mountains through the windowless frames, and bragged that we were the first Irish garrison since that of Patrick Sarsfield.

One of my old London chums turned up at Larkfield a week before Easter Week. Garret MacAuliffe. He was to make his mark in the years to follow in Limerick. I regarded him as my own convert – it was another case in which the pupil outclassed the teacher.

Mick Collins was living with the Plunkett family during this period. Whether he stayed there at night, I do not know. But as Easter Week approached, he was busy about something that I felt was ominous – he was hurried and unusually discourteous. But his attitude, his urgency, was never a bore.

He came into our quarters at the mill on one occasion

when a good deal of fun was going on; we were indus-
triously making grenades. Mick spoke roughly to one of
the 'lambs', who was slotting screws, suggesting he was not
working hard enough, and passed generally abusive remarks.
I suggested Mick should show us how to work faster, put a
three-cornered file in his hand and gave him a bolt-head to
slot. He proceeded to show us how, and a crowd gathered
about him. Of course, the file slipped on the round bolt
head. Meanwhile, I had put half a dozen bolts in a vice and
said, 'Do you think this way might be right, Mick?' I ran my
hacksaw across the half dozen bolts and, 'heigh-presto', six
were slotted. The 'lambs' roared with laughter, and Mick,
swearing at us, went up the stairs to George Plunkett, followed by a gibing chorus of 'The birds of the air fell a sigh-
ing and a sobbing when they heard of the death of poor
Mick Collins ...'

Someone remarked that Mick, as usual, had been treading
in someone else's preserves. Yet I think more than one of us
had noticed his serious, busy demeanour, and sensed he was
nearer to the centre of activities. Of course, none of us were
to know that after his death in action in 1922, those of us
who survived would witness the biggest Irish funeral since
that of Parnell – after a slowly progressing cortege akin to
the one in America for Lincoln. Or that Mick was to prove
our Abraham, or – more aptly – our Moses, leading us in
time to victory and the first independent Irish Free State.

PARADE IN COLLEGE GREEN – 17 MARCH 1916

The Dublin Brigade of the Irish Volunteers paraded in College Green, in full kit and armed, on St Patrick's Day 1916. There were no cheering crowds. Dubliners did not appear interested.

There were four battalions on that parade, including our own, in all perhaps 2,000 men, each man with a lethal weapon, some more deadly than a rifle. A shotgun can be a brutal weapon at close quarters.

The parade took up position in front of the old Irish parliament buildings – nowadays the Bank of Ireland – and it extended along much of Dame Street. Eoin MacNeill was then the figurehead of the Volunteers, and carried out the inspection. One of his aides-de-camp was Barry Mellowes. Both were neatly dressed in uniform. Eoin MacNeill, with his beard and glasses, looked like what he was, a professor. Mellowes looked like a favourite pupil with his glasses and bulging forehead, harmless looking, if one had no sense of history; but these armed men were on historic ground, where once before defiance was proclaimed – as by the last Irish parliament of Henry Grattan.

The British authorities (perhaps unwisely) retained their wonted nonchalance. The whole Dublin Brigade of the Volunteers could have been easily captured that day. But then a university professor is notoriously harmless, and makes an excellent stalking horse, as history was to prove.

INSIDE THE GPO

After the parade, our battalion proceeded to mass at St Audoen's in High Street. The street is very narrow at one point, hardly wide enough for two columns abreast. Just when the Volunteer parade approached the narrow part, a column of British troops appeared; ironically enough, an Irish regiment coming from church-parade on St Patrick's Day. The two columns passed so closely that they all but touched and brushed against each other as they marched to attention. Any private in that British-Irish column must have recognised the significance of armed free-Irishmen – and to their credit they would not have told their employers what they all knew. And so they and we passed in proud silence.

The parade entered St Audoen's. The noise of the rifles as we took our seats struck me as irreverent – as if it was taking the joke too far. Our officers took up position near the front. At the elevation of the Host, they stood to attention with their caps on, drew their swords and saluted. I was struck by the variety of swords. Some were American cavalry swords, others duelling weapons, some dress-swords of the eighteenth century. But they were all very bright and very sharp.

It created a peculiar sensation, that salute of swords, which struck me as either blasphemous or a fanatic vow of fidelity. Those young officers were more religious than I could ever be. If I had not been so emotionally aware, I might not have sensed that it was a portent of something that made me shiver, a premonition of the end, when we would kill each other.

★ ★ ★

Our garrison at Larkfield worked harder after St Patrick's Day. Considering that most of our garrison had been born and bred in the heart of the empire, we were delightfully naive in hoping to challenge the British army. Having spent twelve months near a camp rumoured to hold close to half a million British soldiers near Salisbury, and having seen the effect of artillery training, I preferred not to think about our prospects of success.

More men arrived to swell our garrison, having burnt their boats. Some had openly raided quarries for gelignite, or had captured arms and were known by the RIC. Two Volunteers, Brennan and Peadar Bracken, had opened fire on the RIC when challenged. Bracken was an excellent shot – and I was to see an exhibition of that not much later.

IN SIGHT OF OUR COMMANDER-IN-CHIEF:
P.H. PEARSE

Our company was honoured with an address by Patrick Pearse. He told us we would be specially constituted as 'A Company of Headquarters Battalion', and our duty would be to fight 'under, and in defence of, the Commander-in-Chief'. It was hard to realise that this tall, scholarly man, somewhat stout (with a bad figure resulting from a sedentary life), and a cast in one eye, was our major revolutionary leader. He gave us a lecture on street- and house-fighting. There is no doubt he was an excellent teacher, for his precepts were later carried out to the letter. Pearse spoke slowly, with careful, very measured, cadences. I didn't know then that he was struggling with an habitual stutter, and it did not seem to me that we were all listening to the famous Irish Republican Brotherhood orator who had roused Ireland the year before by the grave of the Fenian leader, O'Donovan Rossa. But here was the same man who had spoken words I had read and knew by heart: 'The fools, the fools, the fools, they have left us our Fenian dead, and while Ireland holds these graves, Ireland unfree shall never be at peace.'

He concluded his address with a reference to our 'allies', and his 'sincere hope for success this time'. I remember feeling doubtful, and taking 'our allies' with a certain amount of salt – a doubt more than justified by the later disasters in County Kerry[10].

We were also inspected by Thomas MacDonagh, who made a bad impression. During his inspection he saw an

---

10 This reference is, among other things, to the Easter-time attempt to land guns from a German submarine in Kerry by Sir Roger Casement, who was hanged at Brixton Prison, 1916, for his involvement in the insurrection. An earlier shipment, though successfully landed at Howth, the small fishing village north of Dublin, proved to be far from first-class equipment, and the German 'allies' were much less than fully committed.

empty porter bottle in the sentry-box, and bawled us off good and solid, telling us how unsoldierly it was *not* to conceal the bottle. He touched us on the raw, as we w ere nearly all abstainers. The empty bottle was our standing joke: 'So That the Sentry was Provided For!' We stood to attention for a long time, and were furious. MacDonagh was right, however; we were not yet soldiers, and never could be, in the professional sense.

A rumour reached us that James Connolly was impatient to go into action. P.H. Pearse, in his address, had implied action in the near future and, to a man, our entire company was eager for it as Easter Sunday was approaching. The whole garrison was enjoined to perform their Easter duties, which we all did – some for the first time in many years, others for the last time ever.

THE EASTER RISING, 1916

EASTER SUNDAY DAWNED. We expected to go into action, but there were no orders. George Plunkett walked about, looking worried. Towards dusk, a car drew up outside our entrance gates. It was immediately approached by a number of men in plain-clothes: detectives. Our armed guard at the entrance forced the detectives to withdraw, and Denis Daly stepped out of the car. Denis said to me, 'It has been a fatal business, Joe – I'll tell you later.' It transpired that Volunteers had been sent to meet Casement in County Kerry, not knowing then that Casement was already arrested. Their car had been driven over a cliff11. We had lost two of our best men – Donal Sheehan and Con Keating – and God knew what else. One of their jobs had been to seize a British

---

11 Off Ballykissane Pier, Killorglin, County Kerry.

wireless-transmitter, so that we could later broadcast news of the Rising to the world.

By Monday morning, the garrison was in a state bordering on insubordination. Eoin MacNeill had called off our Easter parade in Dublin – calculated to mask the start of the Rising – and made a public cancellation of our mobilisation throughout the rest of the country. We were let down, and we thought, some of us, that we'd become rats in a trap. Some spoke of going to join Connolly in Liberty Hall. We were unwashed and angry, and took little notice of poor George Plunkett, who tried to make us clean our quarters. We refused to make our beds. We ate our breakfasts, anyhow. We were at least well stocked. The Cumann na mBan had sent us Easter gifts of cakes, eggs and sweets, the first time we had seen delicacies in months. The Cumann na mBan (or 'Band of Women' – the Volunteers' Women's Auxiliary) had looked wonderful on parade, and I had seen some who were armed to the teeth. They would prove wonderful nurses before the week was over.

Some of the Volunteers were walking about eating cake, others eating pieces of ham. George Plunkett came in and blew his whistle for the fall-in. At first we took no notice of him. He continued to blow his whistle. But moral discipline reasserted itself: we fell in – though still eating what we had in our hands.

George started reading from a dispatch: 'D Company, Headquarters Battalion, will parade at Beresford Place, with full equipment, at the hour of ...' But we heard no more. We burst from our ranks, and dashed for our equipment and arms. George, God rest you, you were a gallant captain of a worthy company.

Our company marched to the tramline and boarded a tram in order to fulfil our mobilisation on time. Honest George Plunkett paid the fares, giving the conductor about ten shillings and saying, 'Fifty-nine twopenny fares – and please don't stop until we reach O'Connell Bridge.' (Some of our number had been detached for action elsewhere.) It had been raining for a fortnight, but that day, I remember, it was bright, warm and sunny, with high clouds in the sky. We were as cheerful as excursionists off to the seaside. The civilian passengers protested, and demanded we be put off the tram. Each of us was carrying bulky equipment, including a rifle or shotgun and a spare pike. I carried a woodsman's axe as an extra. It was handy, and glittered beautifully. Johnny O'Connor had a flute. As 'Blimey' played on his flute, we sang on the top of the open tram. We were jeered at, and cheered back at travellers on the trams passing in the opposite direction.

We arrived at O'Connell Bridge, and then marched down along the Eden Quay by the River Liffey to Liberty Hall, headquarters of the Irish Citizen Army, by Butt Bridge.

We were halted and stood quietly to attention. Above our heads, right across the full facade of Liberty Hall, was a huge banner that proclaimed in bright letters, 'WE SERVE NEITHER KING NOR KAISER – BUT IRELAND!' Gulls wheeled above us, and some curious onlookers gathered to watch. Trams passed, full, en route to the seaside.

I remember especially seeing Joe Plunkett, beautifully dressed with riding boots and spurs, standing in the roadway, going over a plan with a number of our officers round him. Tall, aristocratic, with his *pince-nez* glasses and clever-looking face, he was the picture of the traditional staff-officer. He had a high, stiff collar to his tunic, and a little gold braid. Some wit beside me said, 'Ludendorff'[12]; and I replied, 'Dressed to death.'

It was becoming very warm, and I stepped out of the ranks to throw my collar down the area of Liberty Hall. I felt the collar was superfluous in view of what was imminent.

James Connolly appeared. He looked very drab beside Joe Plunkett, in his ill-fitting, bottle-green, thin serge uniform. The form of dress impressed me as representing two different ideas of freedom. I had seen Connolly before, and was again struck by his unsoldierly appearance. He was rather pot-bellied, with bandy legs and a disorderly moustache. Daniel O'Connell, whose fine baroque monument we'd just passed at O'Connell Bridge, had been a splendid figure of a man. James Connolly was a naked fact. Connolly gave

---

12 Eric von Ludendorff: German general and chief of staff to Hindenberg.

an order and our company started removing loaded cases from Liberty Hall, putting them on to a four-wheeled cab. We handled the boxes very carefully, though I discovered later that they contained – of all things – batons that were later to be issued to some of our men for police-duty.

Then our whole party, including some Citizen Army men, began the march to the General Post Office, Pearse, Connolly and Plunkett marching in front, followed by the four-wheeler. Our own Kimmage Company was in the rear. We went via Abbey Street, which made some sense, as we attracted less attention by that back route than if we had gone via Eden Quay – around the north side of O'Connell Bridge.

There were only two or three of us in uniform, the rest in civilian clothes, a maze of straps and strings. We each had a 'Sam Browne' with two straps – most uncomfortable over a civilian jacket, which bulged everywhere. Towels, soap, candles and spare socks were disposed about our persons or in haversacks, and our blankets were a further heavy encumbrance. When I looked at that swaying, overloaded growler, our 'army transport', tears, I think, were near my eyes. But for that tall figure like Saint Francis, and that little stout man who had said, 'The great only appear great because we are on our knees,'[13] I would have said to my comrades, 'This is foolishness.' But I knew it was about to be bloody, however foolish.

---

13 Connolly had adopted words originally spoken by one of the leaders of the French Revolution, Camille Desmoulins.

INSIDE THE GPO

On our arrival at the General Post Office, we were halted. George Plunkett gave the order 'Into Line – Left Turn!' This brought us into two lines, facing the main entrance to the Post Office. He then called 'A Section, Right Wheel' – and A Section ran round to Henry Street; then he called 'D Section, Left Wheel' – this bringing the section I was in facing south, in the direction of O'Connell Bridge. I then heard George shouting 'B and C Sections – Charge!' The word 'charge' was very quiet, as if he had lost the power to shout. B and C sections immediately swept into the entrance of the GPO. I heard the sound of breaking glass almost instantly – though D Section, of which I was one, was now running towards O'Connell Bridge.

Peadar Bracken was in charge of my section. To where we were running I did not know, but as we were going in the direction of Dublin Castle, I did not want to arrive out of breath. Fortunately, we were halted at O'Connell Bridge.

Peadar placed three men on O'Connell Bridge, with orders to allow none of the enemy to cross the bridge. These three Volunteers were Arthur Agnew of Liverpool on my left, Paddy Moran of Glasgow on the right, and myself – a Londoner – in the middle.

By one of those freaks of circumstance, I was positioned in the centre of the bridge, with my back to the O'Connell statue. I still had my gleaming axe. There was a great deal of noise from the GPO direction. The orders to smash all glass, as per our lectures in street-fighting, to avoid flying splinters, were being carried out, and there was a considerable amount of smashing. Meanwhile, there were three men to hold a bridge – armed only with three shotguns and an axe.

The rest of our section were busy. Some had entered Kelly's Gun Shop (later Kapp and Petersens', of tobacco and pipe fame), and Seamus Robinson was trying to get into Hopkins and Hopkins on the other quayside (Eden Quay) – a hard nut to crack, as it is a jeweller's. Meanwhile I stood in the middle of the bridge, feeling somewhat foolish, on a narrow 'island' between tram-tracks. That central 'island' is still there today, often filled with flowers, though the trams are long gone.

I've measured that bridge since. It's 150 feet across from balustrade to balustrade - maybe the only bridge in the world that, as the joke goes, is even wider than it is wide. Oddly enough, I don't believe I was frightened, at first, but I wondered if either of my pals felt as I did – which was ridiculous. A woman approached me and asked, 'Are the military out after you?'

'No, Madam,' said I. 'The boot is on the other foot.'

I could not take it seriously. Never could, until such time as the streets would be wrecked again, only five years later, in the Civil War.

Meanwhile, the kind woman who had spoken to me returned to me once more, with a large number of small packets of cigarettes – which were later to be a godsend. She was not a mere sympathiser; she was very much with us, and in it up to her neck. Her brother, Captain Weafer, a Volunteer officer, was killed the next day in a burning building.[14]

Another woman approached. She was less friendly to those engaged in warfare. She jeered loudly at me and said, 'Ah, here come the Lancers! Now yew'll see them run!'

Along the quays from downriver was a troop of approaching British Lancers. A second party of Lancers followed – this party appeared to be escorting ammunition. 'Run' was an excellent suggestion – no doubt it would have occurred to me – but how could any man with vanity in him run at the suggestion of a trollop! I stayed put in the middle of the bridge, and my pals on the right and left stayed also.

I felt horribly exposed, however, and called out, 'Will we wipe out this lot, Arthur?' He replied with a wave and a grin.

The leading file of Lancers came abreast of me. I cocked my shot-gun and lined it on the officer, resting the barrel on my arm so that it would not appear too threatening. At one moment, the officer's horse turned in my direction. I all but fired. I did not know if the troop would cross the bridge or continue opposite Bachelor's Walk – west towards the Four Courts[15] – which they very luckily did. I had decided to fire one shot and dive in the river.

---

14 The Imperial Hotel.

15 Garrisoned by Volunteers under command of Ned Daly.

The officer looked at me superciliously with his monocled eye, and the monocle flashed in the light. His troopers were smiling. Meanwhile, glass was crashing everywhere and shots were going off. Seamus Robinson was still smashing in the door of Hopkins and Hopkins, and taking no notice at all of the Lancers passing behind him. For my part, I felt that a hot fermentation had been applied to my feet, and that the heat was passing up my body and out of the top of my head. A little time later, the other troop approached. I was easier in my mind, and stood resting with hands on the axe. The Lancers again smiled. I flourished the axe in salute. It seems that the biggest fools have the best of luck; I had played the clown and got away with it.

'KELLY'S FORT'

Peadar Bracken had entered Kelly's shop. He called out to us on the bridge to come. I entered hurriedly through one of the broken windows – just as I saw Seamus Robinson's party getting into Hopkins and Hopkins. At once we started to barricade windows and doors. I tumbled a beautiful mahogany counter over with a crowbar: it was laden with expensive fishing-tackle. Paddy Moran, beside me, a some-what elderly Glasgow steeplejack, remarked, 'Joe, isn't this awful!' I replied, 'Don't be gentle, Paddy – I'd wipe my nose on the Mona Lisa.'

The housekeeper of the building came on the scene, accompanied by her son, a British soldier on leave. They had been in the flat upstairs. She asked us to spare her little possessions on the top floor. We promised, as surgeons promise, perhaps. The following day, the soldier, a Dubliner, returned demanding a case with his belongings, and I lowered them out of a second-floor window. But by then I'd already extracted from that case a beautiful pair of British officer's brown boots, having exchanged them for my own – which were very uncomfortable. This was hard on the soldier, as he was an officer's batsman, and hard on the officer, no doubt. He asked us again to be careful of his mother's property; alas, I had already tumbled her sewing-machine into the hall on the ground-floor, as part of our barricade.

We had found a large number of books and ledgers, which we used for cover and for forming loopholes; they were very effective. It is hard for bullets to penetrate paper obstructions.

One of our number was placidly filling kitchen utensils with gunpowder and hard objects – the powder from the gun shop's stock, I suppose. He would fill a cast-iron kettle, tie the lid down and put a fuse down the spout; he also possessed an ingenious device made with saucepans. Quite a collection he had at his post by the window.

Peadar Bracken was looking at a rifle and cursing it. It was a German Mauser and rather dirty, more than likely one of the small shipment that had been openly landed by Volunteers at Howth. Peadar had seen action in South America – or so I had heard. It was very probably true. His bad language gave me a feeling of confidence – and foreboding. He was the kind of man who would not wait for things to happen. I had a large number of cigarettes in packets of five, and placed one packet at each window. It was now time to prepare – as per lecture – to burrow from house to house. We needed some heavy tools. There were a lot of roadworker's tools on the far side of O'Connell Bridge. To my surprise, the watchman had not yet deserted. Walking over, I took a number of the tools. Neither of us spoke. I'd selected a heavy specimen. It is strange what a crowbar will reveal.

Theoretically, in house-to-house fighting, one bores from house to house, stepping from one room into the next. It does not work out that way; it's a Lewis Carroll looking-glass experience. One bores a hole at a convenient height, and when the hole is enlarged one prepares to step through – only to find oneself at the ceiling-level of the next apartment, and looking down on a dining table. Worse again, after laborious work one gazes down into the well of a staircase and a hall, the stairs perhaps twelve feet distant below one. Sometimes one unexpectedly breaks in on the privacies of what was a home, and – passing quickly through such apartments – one may conjecture with humour on what difficulties all of this would present to your pursuers.

I saw barricades later that week that were models of ingenuity. In a carpet and linoleum warehouse, the linoleum and
carpets were arranged so that the unwary pursuer could be
buried under an avalanche. Another barricade, stretched across
upper Abbey Street, was made with the entire stock of a bicycle warehouse: thousands of bicycles, piled eight or ten feet
high, jammed into each other. Fire had little or no effect on it.
To cross it on foot was impossible.

The most delightful of all was a barricade of clocks. At last I
saw a use for those horrible marble clocks, like the ones inside
the entrance to a bank. I had seen them in many homes, rarely
keeping or showing the correct time. There were hundreds of
these, barricading a jeweller's door. Alas, there were also some
very beautiful French clocks – but who wanted to know the
time? We had got into our positions. Nothing too seriously
disturbing had happened.

A spare rifle had been found at our outpost at Kelly's Gun
Shop and, as we had no ammunition to suit it, Bracken sent
me with it to the GPO. I set out, using part of the route we
had made by boring through the walls from house to house
towards Abbey Street. A crowd had been swaying for some
time on the street near Nelson's Pillar – I think our improvised policemen had been trying to disperse them. But it
seemed very quiet now. Then, I thought I heard a faint cry
of 'Lancers! Lancers!' Suddenly, a noise like thunder broke
out from the GPO. A troop of Lancers had attempted to

charge. The Lancers had advanced from the north end of O'Connell Street, and suffered some casualties before retreating. I lay prone, afraid to lift my head. Firing seemed to come out of every window. It was some time before I could gain admittance to the GPO, which by this time was very heavily barricaded.

The mood in the Post Office was jubilant after the repulse of that troop of Lancers, but, to my mind, the situation was dangerously chaotic: guns were still going off in all directions by accident. There were some casualties already – mostly from broken or flying glass.

While waiting for a dispatch to take back to our outpost, I had time for a short look about, and had a glimpse or two of our leaders. Connolly was moving from window to window, urging the men to improve their loophole protection. He was also welcoming some late-arriving Volunteers – but there still seemed to me to be very few defenders. Joe Plunkett, looking very pale and ill, was talking quietly to a much older, very frail man. Someone told me it was old Tom Clarke. They were both examining a sheaf of maps or dispatches – and were smiling a lot, with occasional laughter. I didn't see P.H. Pearse, but was told later that he had gone out into the street to read the Proclamation[16.]

---

16 The Proclamation by the Provisional Government of the Irish Republic, read by P.H. Pearse outside the GPO and posted throughout central Dublin on Easter Monday, 24 April 1916.

INSIDE THE GPO

On leaving the Post Office soon afterwards by Prince's Street, I encountered a number of Volunteers with commandeered vans loaded with provisions, struggling to get into the building through milling crowds of onlookers. The crowds were anything but complimentary. Shouts of 'Shitehawks! Lousers! Bowsies!' accompanied me down the street.

EASTER MONDAY EVENING, 24 APRIL

Work continued at 'Kelly's Fort' to prepare our position for defence. Revolution wasn't to begin with marksmanship, but mainly navvies' work. We had to finish our job of knocking down the connecting walls between our post at the river and the next large road, at Abbey Street, a couple of hundred yards away.

During some occasional breaks in our work, from the rooftops we had a clean view of looters on the rampage below us. Clery's Department Store, on the other side of O'Connell Street, was a major casualty. At one time, I had a clear sight of some of our Kimmage lads among a small group of Volunteers, trying to restrain the looters. The populace would pour out from one door, driven by our makeshift peacekeepers, and surge back again into the big shop by another entrance. It was amusing to imagine the tone and accents of some of our Cockney or Liverpudlian admonitions to those celebratory citizens of this newly taken 'Fair City'. To these Dubliners, they would have sounded more alien than the voices of Irishmen in the British army.

The rain returned. A long drizzle continued during our sleepless night. There were frequent short bursts of gunfire from several directions, somewhere south of us in the city. Before dawn – again in the far distance south of the river – came a few distinct, unmistakable, bursts of machine-gun fire.

'The British?' I asked Peadar.

'Must be, I suppose,' he replied. A moment later, he added,' We have no machine-guns.'

TUESDAY, 25 APRIL

The long morning of waiting brought no signs of the British. We were tense with waiting, and anxious to get on with it – whatever *it* might turn out to be. But there were a few distractions.

There were even newspapers to read, brought to us by some messenger or reinforcement from the Post Office. *The Irish Times* had, incredibly, brought out its Tuesday edition, featuring front-page items on the Fairyhouse Races of Monday, and a review of a performance by the D'Oyly Carte Opera Company – who had opened at the Gaiety Theatre the night before. I believe there was an editorial on the Dublin Spring Show at Ballsbridge. I remember (I think) that our '*Sinn Féin Rising* ...' was given a few sentences, with – I believe – a somewhat longer statement from the Dublin Castle[17] authorities that our disturbances were being dealt with effectively. This was not encouraging to men still waiting to be fired upon – and for something to fire back at ...

Somewhat more encouraging was an edition of Connolly's four-page *Irish War News*, fresh from its printing at Liberty Hall, declaring the Republic, and announcing great support from the populace at large, and that the whole centre of the city was in our hands. With these hopeful pages before us, there could be heard the sound of heavy artillery from the north. A few small detachments of Volunteers were passing us, retreating to the Post Office from engagements with British troops to the south. Rumours followed rumours: not all of them were sanguine.

Monday had been difficult to bear, and now Tuesday midday was approaching. The people were indifferent – though with one exception: a man faithfully stood on the street in front of my loophole, very insistently requesting a fishing-rod he had espied – Kelly's Gun Shop was well stocked with sporting goods. I offered him a pike instead – as we had plenty to spare – and asked him if he'd like to join us. He rejected it with scorn, saying, 'Sure that lovely fishin' rod will only be desthroyed, like yourself – it'll never be anny good to you.' This was hard. For both of us. I tried firing

---

17 Headquarters, then, of the British administration in Ireland.

over his head to make him go away, but without avail. He got into a safe corner, out of my sight, and continued to plead, and sometimes curse me.

Looting was on a broad scale by now. From our first-floor window, I threatened some looters carrying jars of sweets, which they then placed on the pavement under me. I turned my head for just a moment and both the looters and the jars disappeared. Once I was offered a new motor-bike for ten shillings by a young boy. He was pushing it away, but, in his own words, 'couldn't sthart the bloody thing!'

And these were the people who, armed with table knives, could annihilate their oppressors? Wasn't it Mitchel, I think, who had written in his *Jail Journal* that 'armed only with kitchen-knives this nation could free itself'? Well, well ... Nothing during those first days of the Rising was to depress the Volunteers more – our leaders and men – than the sometimes senseless and often absurd looting that was occurring in central Dublin. I was less surprised than numbers of my comrades, though many knew better than I the huge scale at that time of the most dismal slum in Europe. The tenements encroached on the delights of every shop-window. If the Volunteers could 'commandeer' what they needed (though paying for what we could, and giving 'receipts' from our Provisional government), couldn't the impoverished citizens of the Dublin slums feel justified – fortified by free booze – in taking their own share, in the absence of any policemen, and before the arrival of the British army?

Later, there were spectacular explosions from upper O'Connell Street, with ascending showers of sky-rockets, star-bursts, Catherine wheels, Roman candles and every imaginable kind of pyrotechnics that a carnival crowd could unleash from a raided toy and fireworks store. This was a bright interruption from the steady, encroaching sounds of heavy fire from our southerly outposts already engaged with the British. Meanwhile, the rape of property all about us went on undiminished.

But everywhere, in those first days of the Rising – and often at the most tense and difficult times later in that week – the Volunteers and Citizen Army men sang and were merry. I got promotion later for singing – I did not deserve it for merriment.

Meanwhile, I'd found a fine sword at our outpost, and on my next journey with messages to the GPO, took it with me to give to Mick Collins. On my way, I found the pavement littered with stiff, starched collars the looters had no use for; it's hard to march through a street carpeted with stiff collars, and it was a strain on my dignity as I walked along, carrying my shotgun and sword.

An old lady, one of the looters still as busy as termites in the streets, perhaps sensing my embarrassment, struck me in the face with a rotten red cabbage. She was about to follow up her attack. If I'd threatened her with my gun, it would not have stopped her. I drew the sword and slashed – intending to clear her head. She fell on her knees – and to my horror something rolled on the pavement. It was her high toque. She begged for mercy and showered silver napkin rings on the pavement from her apron. I marched on – as shaken as she was.

Mick Collins was on the ground floor of the GPO, and I believe now had the stripes of a staff captain; so it was appropriate, it seemed to me, that I give him this sword. He looked hard at me, but accepted my peace offering; I had teased him a good deal at our camp at Larkfield.

On my brief look around the Post Office before leaving, I was struck by the large contingent of women of the Cumann na mBan who had now joined us. They were all wonderfully cheerful-looking in their bright highly coloured sashes, some with Red Cross aprons, others in full fighting kit, their belts stuffed with knives or even big pistols. As I was leaving, Connolly passed me, uttering encouraging shouts, his voice gruff in spite of his smiling face. He appeared, from what I managed to hear, to be taking a detachment to reinforce some nearby outposts.

I hurried back to 'Kelly's Fort' through pouring rain. We settled in for another tense night. I remember wondering how long it would now be before the enemy had possession of those buildings facing us, across the Liffey on the south quays.

INSIDE THE GPO

Some of us managed to sleep in little snatches, between alerts of nearer gunfire. It was the last sleep any of us had for many days to come, and for some, the last sleep before they slept forever. I know I would not have slept much if I had known that in those buildings that faced us, a few hundred yards beyond the Ha'penny Bridge, lay the Telephone Exchange, a vital position we had (by some lunacy of bad planning) neglected or failed to take.

WEDNESDAY, 26 APRIL

Early on Wednesday morning at 'Kelly's Fort', as all were now calling it, we had a big shock. We came very suddenly alert with the crash of shellfire somewhere down river: something very heavy by the sound of it. Our nearest outpost on the other corner of the O'Connell Bridge had begun blazing away with shotguns at something – but what it was we could not see. The shelling sounded loud enough to be a fifteen-pounder. It was, as we were to discover later in the day. The British had brought a gunboat up the Liffey to below Butt Bridge, and were shelling Liberty Hall. Liberty Hall was the headquarters of Connolly's Citizen Army, and of his long-formed Transport and General Workers' Union. We were amazed and shaken by the enemy turning their biggest guns on us so soon, though I was not so surprised as my companions. James Connolly was probably as well known to the

British as our old Fenian leader, Tom Clarke; and Connolly's building must have seemed an obvious and easy target to an adversary that didn't yet know with whom or what it was engaged. Luckily, Liberty Hall was not occupied by any of our insurgents, but it had printed its last communiqué. It was reduced to a husk. Only its outer walls remained by the end of that week, the proud banner of the Citizen Army still hanging on its facade.

It was not until that morning that a shot was fired directly at our post. We'd had plenty of chocolate to eat, but little else. Our position had been reinforced by another five men who had already been in action on the north side of the city. They were country men, healthy and strong, looking fine in their uniforms, and they gave confidence to our small group, who were worn out with watching and waiting. We heard from them that the British had already used artillery in actions against us in the middle-class or poorer districts of Phibsboro or the North Strand.

The first preparations for the British attack against our outpost at 'Kelly's Fort' came from across the river in D'Olier Street, from across O'Connell Bridge, somewhat diagonal to our position. A number of British soldiers calmly came out into the middle of the roadway, about three hundred yards away, and proceeded to deposit tools and all manner of things. They were obviously about to mount a gun, and had begun preparations for lifting the stones – the road there was still cobblestoned for tram tracks. They had stripped off their coats, looking quite workmanlike. Peadar Bracken and those who could do so from their positions fired. Some of the soldiers fell, I believe – I couldn't see from my position. One soldier later put his head round the corner and tried to pull in his comrade. But Peadar's accurate shooting stopped him.

It was quiet for a while. Then bullets were coming into the room from God knows where – they were firing at us with what seemed to be 'pom-pom'. Then they fired tracers. I assumed they were tracer bullets, because when they struck the walls behind you they exploded with a blue flash. Unnerving. You thought you were being attacked in the rear. But our ledgers stood up splendidly to rifle-fire, and even machine-gun fire – which soon followed.

I was coming down the banisterless stairs when the first shell shook our building. It was only a 4.7 – a nine-pounder – but it shook the old house and plaster fell all over the place. With the explosion, I was nearly pitched forward on to my head when I entered the room where the defenders were. That first shell had landed immediately under Peadar on the lower floor.[18]

As the shelling of our position intensified, Peadar Bracken ordered the men to retire, but he stayed himself, looking through a loophole. Not that there was anything to see. The gun firing

---

18 Numerous shell-holes in the face of the building can easily be seen in a photograph taken from the other side of O'Connell Bridge after the Rising was over.

at us seemed to be lobbing its shells from over the buildings on the other side of the bridge; we guessed from somewhere at the further end of D'Olier Street. The British were by now occupying the houses directly opposite, on the other side of the River Liffey. We continued trying to return their fire, but the short range of shotguns (Peadar had the only rifle) gave us little chance of hitting anything. Also, with every blast from a further shell our views were obscured, even from each other, by the clouds of dust and falling plaster. The chances of our getting any shots back in answer shrunk as we came under increasing fire − including machine-guns − from the opposite side of the river. As the afternoon wore on, Peadar Bracken was still at his window, though with the dust and smoke from the bombardment we could see very little.

'We are cut off,' I said to Peadar, 'I think our lads have now retired from the other side of the road.'

In fact, though they *had* withdrawn from Hopkins and Hopkins, on misunderstood orders from James Connolly, they were to return and put up a hell of a fight there until very late in the week. But at that time, we couldn't be sure that they were still holding on our left flank.

Peadar said to me, 'We have no orders to retire. Tell the lads they can come back.'

'I could reach Headquarters,' said I. 'This appears hopeless to me.'

'All right,' said Peadar, 'we'll give that a try.'

SORTIE TO THE GPO

He came with me to nearly the end of our block of build-ings, through which we had extended by knocking holes in the connecting internal walls. I had put on a very long black coat and a round clergyman's hat, reversing an ordinary stiff collar. I dropped from a high wall into a back lane. I've looked at that drop since. It's said that fear lends wings to the feet. I can add 'and parachutes'.

I came into Abbey Street, which was – amazingly – deserted and silent. It was a grand feeling to have the sky for a ceiling. I ventured to enter a boot shop, Mansfield's, in the first building of the block adjoining the GPO. There was a burst of machine-gun fire poured into it, which made me jump back hurriedly. I was not then familiar with Dublin; I did not yet know that there is a small courtway leading to the GPO from Abbey Street to Prince's Alleyway. I walked past it for about two hundred yards, to the corner of the street, where there was a pub. There were men still in that pub, drinking pints. One man told me to retrace my steps and I would find the small courtway leading to the side entrance of the Post Office. He then very pleasantly advised me not to hurry my pace, as the street was under observation by 'them milithary in Capel Street'. He added, sizing up my garb and after a brief glance at my face above its clerical collar, 'You look pale, Father.' I was relieved that he thought me a priest.

I didn't trouble to disenchant him. I certainly *felt* pale, and needed the drop of port wine he gave me. And I didn't know whether to be sorry or glad when directed to my objective. I slowly retraced my steps until I saw the entrance to the courtway I needed; then I remembered my brown boots – incongruous with my clerical garb – and that the British must have field-glasses trained on the street, and fled.

On reaching the GPO, I reported the position of my company and was ordered to tell them to withdraw. As to what exactly happened then, I am not clear. I know I got back to our outpost and have a recollection of calling for them wildly. Again I entered Abbey Street, and saw a civilian who informed me that he had seen a group of men crossing the road with pikes and crowbars. God knows why he was hanging about there, but he put my mind at rest. Once more I returned to the GPO, where I met my pals from 'Kelly's Fort'.

Our captain, George Plunkett, said that our post should not have been abandoned; that he had been back there himself, and said it could be occupied again. I was doubtful. It was suggested that a barricade be put across the road at Abbey Street, so that the block of buildings could be reoccupied.

The method was simple enough. Baskets on wheels were loaded and packed tight with newspapers and journals; these were to be run out, one after another, from a shop, to form a barricade across the road – and I was to push out the first hamper. Fortunately, there was an inclined plane leading from the shop into Abbey Street. I pretended to slip, and let my wheeled basket enter the street. It was cut to bits by machine-gun fire. We shut and barricaded the door, withdrawing towards the GPO.

By now many fires were raging in O'Connell Street. It was still called Sackville Street then, but in remembering anything of that week one always thinks of it as O'Connell Street. A number of the biggest buildings were alight opposite the Hotel Metropole and the GPO. Incendiary shells or fire-bombs were being lobbed into them from somewhere or other; but Volunteers were still firing toward the river from many of the burning buildings.

On our return to the Post Office, the garrison there seemed to my mind unduly optimistic. Those who had been in the GPO during the whole period since noon on Monday had settled down, and some of them had formed their own messes. Desmond Fitzgerald was in charge of the commissariat and the canteen. He served up very meagre rations, saying that he had 'supplies for only ten days or thereabouts'. I'd great doubts myself by then of our holding out for ten days or anything close to 'thereabouts'. And meanwhile, like the rest of my comrades, I was desperately hungry, having not had a real meal since Easter Sunday. Also, perhaps because I had spent much of 1915 near a British military camp in Salisbury Plain, I was bemused by the general attitude of security.

I was soon posted to the first floor of the Metropole, and later to the top floor, in charge of about twelve young lads. Some of these were not Volunteers, but pupils from P.H. Pearse's school of St Enda's, and some civilians who had asked to join in the fight. I was to learn later that we had some very curious European allies: two Swedish sailors and one Spaniard were manning guns in the GPO, though the story going the rounds was that the Swedes had offered to fight only until Thursday – when their boat was due to sail.

'COMRADE', OUR 'UNKNOWN WARRIOR'

There was one older man, an American, who appeared particularly daring. Every now and then, he stepped out on the balcony to assess what might be going on. There were horses loose in the street, and they were running up and down. It was unlikely that they were the mounts of those Lancers who had challenged our defenders on Monday; some dead horses that had been Lancers' mounts were lying close by Nelson's Pillar. These other horses may have escaped from a stable west of our building. Their panicky gallop sounded for a moment (to me) alarmingly like cavalry.

This American continued to offer himself as lookout at any opportunity and, as I felt he was taking my responsibility, I more than once remonstrated with him. But he always got there before me, and addressed me cheerfully as 'Comrade'.

He was not one of the Volunteers, or an Irishman, but an American and a revolutionary who had asked if he might join us. I recognised him at first by his accent, though I had met him only once before – and briefly – as far back as 1913, when he was speaking on a platform at Hyde Park Corner in London on behalf of the IWW (the International World Workers).

He was to die fighting with us and for us, but we do not know where he is buried, and I have never found out his name, though I think he may later have been honoured by the erection of a plaque to his memory in Limerick city. He was our gallant 'Unknown Warrior'.

When I saw him that time in Hyde Park, speaking elo-quently, and obviously with first-hand acquaintance, of the 'Wobblies' – or IWW – he looked hungry and sounded hoarse. He needed a question that would give him some useful openings. I put a couple to him – and was then promptly invited on to his box. This I declined, but the good-natured Londoners bought his pamphlets when I passed them round. It was the nasal American tone in his voice that made me recognise him now, in the Hotel Metropole, under heavy fire from 'imperialist' forces.

He told me that he had reported to Liberty Hall, looking for James Connolly, when the fighting began – he'd obviously known of Connolly as an international socialist, though he insisted that he was unaware of our Volunteer revolutionary movement. A woman of the Cumann na mBan, who had been left behind by Connolly to direct latecomers at Liberty Hall, asked him why he was there, and he said that he was looking for Connolly. She asked him why. When he told her he wanted to join in our revolution, she said, 'We don't need the assistance of an Englishman.' He had enjoyed this accusation, he told me, because he'd never before, in several countries, been taken for anything other than an American.

Later, during the evacuation of our men from the Metropole to the GPO, he was hit by a tracer-bullet, which exploded a big haversack of ammunition which he insisted on carrying and had refused to abandon. He was to die from a great loss of blood, but not until after our surrender. I'll always be glad I was able to be with him almost to the end.

PROMOTION TO THE METROPOLE

For some reason Oscar Traynor, who had now been promoted by Connolly to command the Metropole, told me to take charge of the top floor of the Metropole building. I'd always believed I could sing, and he was the first man who took advantage of it: I was told that the lads there wanted cheering up. As I entered the first room, I was silhouetted against the wall and I got a warning shout from the windows.

It was awe-inspiring. The red glare of the burning buildings opposite lighted the rooms. It was no wonder that the lads were depressed, at that height and looking at an inferno all day long, and now night was falling without darkness. We sang a few songs together, but they remained despondent. Perhaps Traynor's faith in me, at least in that department, was less than well founded.

There were twelve of them, mostly young boys, and they lay there quietly at their posts, not talking to each other. I spoke to them one by one, and concluded by asking them, 'Do you think you are going to die?' Each of them answered, 'I suppose so, Sir.' I told them all to fall in, in the corridor outside the room. One of our flags was flying at our corner of the Post Office. I got them in line facing the flag, and gave the 'Present Arms'. Then I said, 'Lads, you have done that in accordance with tradition. You're now free to go back and die – but I'm damned if I'm going to do so.'

There was a roar of laughter from the young fellows; they had been left too long looking at that holocaust. I took care not to look at it at all.

After some efforts I got a meal for them. They had not eaten for a long time. I kept them all in the largest room and ignored the windows for the greater part of the time. They became cheerful and forgot their fears. But those whom I allowed to sleep gave an occasional sad little sigh or moan.

One loses the distinction between night and day under such conditions. Fortunately the wind was blowing the fire away from the building we were manning, but it could now be only a matter of time before the Hotel Metropole was also engulfed in flame. The GPO seemed to be the last large building in O'Connell Street not yet on fire.

Perhaps song is contagious. It sounded later as if 200 voices were raised from the GPO in some rousing choruses of our 'Soldier's Song'[19]. Mick Collins told me later that it was James Connolly's lusty bellow that got them started. Mick later complained that it spoiled his last chance of any sleep that week.

19 By Peadar Kearney, later to be adopted as the Irish national anthem.

RETURN TO THE GPO

BY EARLY THURSDAY morning, 27 April, I'd been assigned a new post by the Prince's Street corner of the GPO, though occasionally I'd be sent elsewhere throughout the building. Within the Post Office itself there was still, amazingly, an air of some security. Our quartermaster, Desmond Fitzgerald, spoke of having rations for so many days – or weeks – but was unduly niggardly with what he issued. Some of my Kimmage Company pals had laid in a good stock of food, and lived like fighting-cocks. They did me proud.

Our headmasterly leader, P.H. Pearse, was in the main hall on the ground floor, and he was very approachable. The Volunteer privates took every opportunity to have a word with him, like schoolchildren with a favourite teacher.

But it was the courage of Connolly, more than any other leader, which held the men together, though they all looked exhausted – tense from the long wait for the

British infantry attack. A number of his Citizen Army members were to be seen occasionally. They seemed to be detailed for special duties. They were all very good shots and efficient snipers, and were called for, for this service, as one would perhaps call for artillery. They were hard-bitten men: far better to have with you than against you, veterans of South Africa and economic wars, not accustomed to requesting omelettes – but with the knowledge of their making. Unlike most of the rest of us, they were trained and prepared to kill. They'd be a great bulwark when the British infantry attack came, if it ever did. It seemed to me that the British had decided to finish the job with shells and incendiaries, though they got close enough once or twice.

Early in the day, every gun in the Post Office opened up when the British attempted to burst out from Upper Abbey Street, screened for a time by the smoke from the massive fires that were raging. The firing from our position by the Prince's Street corner was very sustained, and there was the comfort of seeing some khaki forms in retreat.

Amazingly, during a lull in the firing, a civilian approached my loophole and asked, repeatedly, if he could enter and join in this battle! By now, we were so nervous and suspicious I trained my gun on him, while my fellow Volunteer, Sean Gallogly, went to Connolly to ask if the man could be admitted. Our aspiring recruit insisted that

I could trust him, saying, 'You needn't be afraid.'

'You're the one should be afraid,' I advised him, 'while *I'm* at the end of this gun!'[20] My shotgun was somewhat hair-triggered.

Much to my surprise, Connolly soon arrived, and then listened to our enthusiast for some moments, before shaking his head and telling him, 'Go home while you can, man, but we thank you. Too late now, man; it's a hopeless cause!' He had spoken sadly and very quietly. He could not have known that either Gallogly or myself might have heard him.

And yet, within a short time of that event, I was to see James Connolly repeatedly leading sorties from the Post Office with men who had volunteered to go with him and reinforce our other positions or establish new ones. Tireless, even when later wounded in the arm and with a shattered ankle, Connolly showed that his energy and courage were indefatigable.

★ ★ ★

I was ordered by Liam Daly to repair the telephone wires on the roof of the GPO. I made the repair hurriedly and lay very flat, hoping my posterior would not be observed above the low balustrade. There were two men on that roof with a

20 This incident, typical of Joe Good, is also recorded in Agony at Easter by Thomas M. Coffey (Penguin 1970).

rotten job. They were very exposed, with just a few sandbags and a tarpaulin for cover. One was Denis Daly. It occurred to me that he could easily be forgotten if – or when – the GPO was set afire.

My friend and fellow-electrician Johnny 'Blimey' O'Connor had done a fine job. He had installed at least basic key communication points throughout the building, including this line to the roof of the Post Office, so James Connolly could maintain some contact with his sharpshooters, the hard-bitten Citizen Army men, who were even now engaged with some British targets east of us across O'Connell Street.

Johnny told me a bitter tale of his two or three days' attempt to restore some defunct wireless apparatus that had been found in a nearby building – the disengaged wireless equipment of the Telephone Company School, on the opposite side of the road. Johnny and his comrades had finally been able to get it running, but very weakly, with maybe just enough wattage to allow at least a few tapped-out Morse code messages to the outside world. We might have been the first insurrectionists to proclaim a new republic anywhere in the twentieth century. Johnny O'Connor said somewhat wistfully that this 'might have been managed, Joe, it really might'. Keeping my backside well down on the roof, I could not help cursing our ineptitude in failing to take possession of the Telephone Exchange near the Liffey on the previous

Monday. We could have cut all enemy communications, and improved our chances of holding out longer.

I was glad to escape back from that roof. The Metropole beside us was by then beginning to burn and shells were landing on it.

I came down from the roof of the Post Office and through the instrument room on the top floor, where Mick Collins was in charge. I looked down at him for a few moments. I hadn't seen him since the previous Tuesday, when he was still active on the ground floor. But this instrument room was secure, having no windows looking out on the street: it was a post of little honour or danger. He looked bad-tempered: a case of Achilles sulking in his tent, perhaps, though Mick, unlike Achilles, was eager for battle.

Mick was a bad junior officer. Respected but not loved by the Kimmage garrison, they could see through some of the tricks he had learned abroad. He was a man of action, and very rough-tongued, but his simulated anger had been much more effective in England. Though it would work wonders yet in Ireland. All through this week he gave me the impression that he was in a post that was too minor for a man of his temperament. But his time was yet to come. A while later Mick had work a bit more to his liking – trying to put out a fire. Joe Reilly was working beside him. Mick's trousers caught fire and Joe put it out by hosing Mick down. Mick, as ever, was furious.

Machine-gun fire directed against us in the Post Office was by now often sustained. During the brief lulls in the firing, we felt the heat of encroaching flames, accompanied by dense smoke across the 150 feet of O'Connell Street, causing us to feel deeper discouragement.

On my return to the ground floor, I was astonished to find that a large number of the men were singing – none too loudly, but doing their best to match the big voice of a sturdy, handsome Volunteer commander with an amazingly cheerful countenance decorated with a formidably waxed moustache.

'Who is *that*?' I asked a young country lad near to me.

'O'Rahilly – sure that's *The* O'Rahilly!' said he delightedly. 'He's been treating us to a few songs, and this is one of his *own*!

So this was Michael O'Rahilly. 'The' O'Rahilly. Author of songs I'd first heard and learned in London-Irish halls, singing his own 'Thou Art Not Conquered Yet, Dear Land' – against this background of advancing flames and gunfire:

'Though knaves may scheme and slaves may crawl
To win their master's smile,
And though thy best and bravest fall,
Undone by Saxon guile –

Yet some there be, still true to thee,
Who never shall forget
That though in chains and slavery
Thou art not conquered yet!'

Hearing that, from the mouth of the man who had written it and was now singing it, made my fifty-shilling ticket from England very much more worthwhile.

I'd had very mixed feelings about O'Rahilly – we all had – but that one sight and sound of him made him for ever 'The' O'Rahilly for me. 'The O'Rahilly' was a title he had assumed as head of some famed County Kerry clan. He had founded our Volunteer movement. With hindsight, now, I know that though he'd been a senior officer in our organisation – and not on the inner council of the IRB – he'd not been consulted on our leaders' decision to launch this Rising from the Easter Sunday parade. We all knew that, with MacNeill, he had countermanded our full mobilisation, and over the Easter weekend had toured the country, expending every effort to see that the cancellation was obeyed. We knew he was of the moderate Volunteer alignment that was convinced a Rising at this time was disastrously mistimed. But once he'd found that the insurrection was on, in spite of all efforts to stop it, he'd arrived for our muster on that Monday at Liberty Hall. And we all knew what he'd said to Pearse and Connolly, something that one of our lads from

INSIDE THE GPO

Kimmage had overheard: 'I helped wind this clock and I've come to hear it strike.'

SHELLING OF THE GPO – WORDS FROM P.H. PEARSE

The first British shells now struck. The Metropole Hotel was ablaze and Traynor's men had been withdrawn, though they returned to it later and remained in action there. Connolly led yet another sortie from the Post Office and was brought back with a shattered ankle. Our numbers were increasing, with the arrival of groups of Volunteers forced to retreat from burning buildings in O'Connell Street and other outposts.

At some time that afternoon, the men were called together and assembled for an address by Patrick Pearse. He read a communiqué – quite a long one – that was difficult to hear for those left posted at the windows, of which I was one. I could catch only a few phrases. We were, he said, 'making arrangements for the final defence of headquarters and are determined to hold it while our buildings last'. He wanted to thank us for our gallantry, in case he might not be given an opportunity to do so later. He praised us for fighting for four days and nights without rest or sleep or any complaint. The men were told that they deserved to win – that 'win it they will although they may win it in death'.

His voice rose nearer the end of his speech – which we could hear more clearly – insisting that we had all *'redeemed*

Dublin from shame and made her name splendid among the names of cities!' He finished by asserting that the Irish Republic had been established by our actions and that his government had attained the right to be at a 'peace table' by the end of the war in Europe.

I wasn't too hopeful of that. Yet, in spite of some words like 'winning in death' and 'final defence', there was an amazing and spontaneous cheer as the men moved back to their positions.

And yet, as time dragged on, our morale would have begun to weaken, I'm sure, if it hadn't been for Joe Plunkett. Pearse seemed to have shot his bolt; Connolly, gravely wounded, was at that time out of action and out of sight. But Joe moved amongst us all the time, his eloquent, comforting words at odds with his bizarre, eccentric appearance, his dangling sabre and jewelled fingers. We all, somehow, and in many differing ways, responded to his gentle urgings and praise. He was greatly loved.

Most of us by now knew that he'd risen from his deathbed to lead us: Mick Collins had had to help to get him dressed on Monday morning. Joe's high uniform-collar didn't any longer quite hide that bandaged throat from his operation of only a few days before. He was already dying of a galloping consumption.

Joe Plunkett realised, I felt, that the engulfing flames around us were far more frightening than machine-gun and shell fire. He said to one of our officers near by, with his typical surge of excitement: 'It's the first time this has happened since Moscow! The first time a capital city has burned since 1812!'

FRIDAY, 28 APRIL – CONNOLLY'S MESSAGE

Our last day in the Post Office had come. There had been some sporadic gunfire during the night – I think some of our outposts were still in action. O'Rahilly was tireless during those earliest hours before dawn. He led countless parties of us to remove all manner of explosives from the upper floors and even the roof – dynamite and large amounts of ammunition.

The fires opposite had died down somewhat, leaving blackened hulks of buildings. Gunfire of all kinds had abated. We were all convinced that the long-awaited infantry attack by the British was now at hand. We were still piling up higher breastworks before the ground-floor windows as Connolly was moved amongst us, sitting up on his bed, which was being rolled along on castors. He was joking and laughing – almost as if he was back in direct command. He had himself wheeled to a position from which most of us could see him. His secretary, Miss Kearney, was still – as always – beside him. We were told that he'd written a message for all of us. The O'Rahilly stood beside him to read it out. The O'Rahilly did him proud.

That was the most amazing thing I witnessed that week. It was an extraordinary communiqué considering the situation we were in and what lay before us. We were welcomed to the fifth day of the 'New Republic', and told that our other commandants were still holding out with their men in the other insurgent strongholds. We were all reminded that for the *'first time in seven-hundred years'* the flag of a free country floated above our heads. Connolly's words saluted our other active commandants throughout Dublin: he spoke of de Valera and MacDonagh, Daly and Kent[21]. The long message finished with 'Courage boys – we are winning!' He had praise for our women of the Cumann na mBan, some of whom were standing among us.

EVACUATION OF THE WOMEN

But, shortly after that, word went round that all the girls were to be gathered in the main hall. I was very surprised that there were so many; between twenty and thirty young women were assembled before Patrick Pearse, who spoke briefly to them. I watched as they were told that the time had come when they must go. Some of the girls burst into tears, but the majority of them were very angry, and shouted back at him, refusing to leave ... 'No! – No! – We'll stay with the men!' ... 'You told us we were all equal!' ... 'What about women's rights?'

---

21 Eamonn Ceannt.

Pearse was very obviously shaken, and did not know how to handle the situation, which was very clearly now getting out of hand. Little Sean MacDermott – he was stricken with polio – limped over, leaning on his cane, and appeared to cancel Pearse's order. Not really a small man – I've been told since that MacDermott once had a superb physique, and was in his youth quite an athlete, but his earlier imprisonment had resulted in polio, from the effects of which, despite an enormous cheerfulness, he'd never recovered. Unlike Joe Plunkett, who was terminally ill, MacDermott possessed the same almost superhuman vitality as Mick Collins. He was the only man I've ever seen who reminded me of Collins.

Pearse, it seemed, must have insisted on the departure of the women, for shortly afterwards, still protesting, they very reluctantly moved towards a door. A Red Cross flag was raised before them and, after another delay, they were finally ushered out into Henry Street. Mercifully, there was a short lull in the firing. The men were silent. We were all relieved – but very sorry to see them go.

INCENDIARY SHELLING

The first incendiary shells were soon exploding on the roof. Mick Collins and O'Rahilly led us in an effort to quench the flames. It was hopeless, as the water pressure in the very old hoses gradually ran out. But every man who could be spared from a defence position was engaged in trying to hold back the inferno, including Sean MacDermott and Tom Clarke. But we were forced back into the ground floor. MacDermott led a big section of men who were by then transferring our stocks of explosives to the basement.

Machine-gun fire was coming in the first floor, and some men were wounded. The storey above was ablaze by now. Men were being withdrawn from the windows, and an attempt was made to erect another barricade further back, near the courtyard; but this was later abandoned. Strangely, in these circumstances, we salvaged a big stock of tobacco.

The room was flooded with water with fire floating on it. One young Volunteer remained at the windows. I told him to withdraw. He said he had received no order. A gentle little man, the butt of his comrades' jokes at Larkfield, he remarked to me, 'Joe, this is getting serious.' So, we also had our simple lad who could owe God a death[22] and not complain.

The enemy appeared to have closed in. There were bursts of machine-gun fire through the ground-floor windows. And their snipers found some more targets. The Volunteers had 'fallen in' outside in the courtyard. One iron staircase into the basement remained, though the building was burning badly. Men were bringing up bags of bread; a Volunteer in the ranks fell wounded.

---

22 Henry IV, part 2.

Three members of our Cumann na mBan – some of our nurses had remained – were turning over an assortment of gaily coloured silk scarves for bandages, and to a remark I made, one man replied, 'Ah, there's the "Eternal Feminine".'

A party of us were detailed to take our rather dangerous hand-grenades down to the basement. Some of these were round tins filled with shrapnel. This job was carried out calmly, although some sparks were falling down the lift-shaft into the basement, which O'Rahilly was still hosing down. One man, seeing the danger, left his hand-grenades on the stairs and did not complete his journey.

Some of our wounded were being evacuated – I think via the buildings behind us to Jervis Street Hospital. A small group of Cumann na mBan girls who had remained to accompany them were accepting farewell messages for their families. Tom Clarke approached and spoke to a girl. He said, I remember, 'If you see my wife, tell her that the men fought ...' He was unable to finish, and turned away. I moved away myself, embarrassed that I might be thought to be eavesdropping, although my overhearing of the words spoken was entirely unintentional.

Pearse had called us together and selected a group of men for a special duty. I felt glad that he passed me over. He spoke to them briefly. Word spread quickly that they would be our vanguard party under The O'Rahilly, who would try to break through the enemy and get us to another building called William and Woods.

There was then a very long wait. It seemed as if the intention might be to delay our departure until daylight had faded. It was dusk by now, but I thought our departure would be as dangerously obvious in the glare of the burning building as it would be in broad daylight. Someone had burst into 'The Soldier's Song', and soon every voice, it seemed, was raised in chorus – 'So-oldiers are we ...' – among shards of falling, burning timbers. It was time – high time, I thought – for us to go.

The beginning of a more peaceful time of life – a wedding photograph of Joe Good and Mary Ellen Donovan.

Above: The centre of the second city of the British Empire – Sackville Street, Dublin, seen from across O'Connell Bridge.

Below: The grand interior of the General Post Office, Sackville Street.

Left: Joseph and Count Plunkett in 1908.

Below: A group of rebels photographed inside the GPO during the Easter Rising (from left to right): Desmond O'Reilly, James Mooney, Paddy Byrne, John Doyle, Tom McGrath, Hugh Thornton, John J Twamly, and Bernard Frick.

Four of the architects of the Rising (clockwise from top left):
Patrick Pearse, James Connolly, Sean MacDermott and Tom Clarke.

Left: Michael Collins, with whom Joe Good worked and fought closely throughout the revolutionary years.

Irish Rebellion – May 1916.
Holding a Dublin street against the Rebels.

Above: British soldiers defending a barricade, constructed from some benches and barrels and a butcher's block.

Joe Good with two comrades-in-arms, Johnny 'Blimey' O'Connor and Ernie Noonan.

Above: Heavy artillery being wheeled up a Dublin street.

Right: The view of Sackville Street across O'Connell Bridge after the Rising, with the O'Connell monument and the ruins of the DBC restaurant.

6719-11   THE SINN FEIN REVOLT IN DUBLIN.   ROTARY PHOTO. E.C.
GENERAL VIEW SHOWING RUINED D.B.C. RESTAURANT.

Above: An armoured lorry hastily assembled for the British during the Rising.

Below: Another view across O'Connell Bridge to the ruins of Sackville Street.

WITHDRAWAL
FROM THE GPO

P.H. PEARSE WAS standing at the exit to Henry Street, with what appeared to be plans in his hand. One wondered at the plans. A wounded man on a stretcher was blocking the exit, and it was difficult to extricate him. There was a press of men behind him. Eventually they stepped over him. Later two of us were to carry him and put him in a position of relative safety. There was considerable firing from the enemy down Henry Street. But though there was something of a crush, there was no panic. However, during this time a number of shotguns were accidentally discharged and a couple of men were wounded. I helped carry a wounded man and arrived near the rear of the main party, where we were forced to halt.

There was considerable confusion in Henry Place. Rifle-fire was coming from a whitewashed house a few yards distant, which halted our retreat. As our men were passing this house, there was fire from five or six rifles, some of them our own 'Howth' rifles I assumed, because the explosions were very loud[23]. This house was held by our own men, but they did not know who were approaching and thought we were the British. We were crouched in a small space. I got into a corner beside a telegraph-pole and watched.

There were shouts of 'You are firing on your own men' from our party, but the firing persisted. I saw one or two men fall while trying to pass the house. Our advance was halted. Some Volunteers tried to break down a nearby door with the butts of their rifles, and shot the men behind them – one at least was shot in the head or neck, and dropped like a stone. One or two Volunteers had left a cartridge in the breech; their safety catches were off or had been shaken off.

Connolly was left on his back in the middle of the road near the whitewashed house, alone and shouting. At some point a small man – it was my friend Johnny O'Connor – persuaded some of the men to lift him and put him through a small window, after which he opened a door from inside. But we were still pressed into a small space, and there was some confusion. I took it upon myself to approach Pearse

---

23 The German rifles landed at Howth exploded like cannons. With homemade Volunteer bullets, they were (as Joe often said) more lethal to those who fired them than the enemy at whom they were aimed.

and suggest to him that a rearguard be placed at the bottom of Moore Lane facing the GPO. He agreed to this and it was carried out: having no rearguard until then, we would have been cut to pieces had any cavalry come.

Some of our military prisoners, whom we had captured during the week, appeared terrified – as was natural in the confusion – being lined up as they were against a wall. The whites of one officer's eyes could be seen by me ten yards away. There seemed to be a lot of white – but he was a brave man and had proved it. I suggested to O'Rahilly that they be let go to take their chances on escaping. It looked to me as if we were trapped; but he misunderstood me, and thought I was suggesting using them for cover, and he almost struck me. Then he saw my point and apologised, and let them go.

CHARGE OF THE O'RAHILLY

We put the Volunteer whom we had been carrying on a stretcher inside the doorway of Hamilton Long's, the chemists. When I came out, I heard O'Rahilly calling for twenty men to follow him in a charge with rifles and bayonets. There was not a very prompt response to his call, which seemed reasonable to me, because who or what he was going to charge was not clear, unless he intended to charge that white house – which seemed unlikely. But one man stepped out at once, well-equipped. He was to die and had said so to me days before. Two or three dropped their rifles.

Whom (or where) they were going to charge I still could not see. Mick Collins approached me and asked was it my rifle lying on the ground. I said no – I had never had one. Perhaps it did not occur – to either of us – that it was there for the taking.

Meanwhile, gunfire was still coming from the white house in bursts. They were our own men, made more suspicious by the prisoners in British uniform who had run past. I thought I could find a hand-grenade to throw into the white house, although there was little doubt in my mind as to who occupied it. I asked Pearse, I think, where I could get a hand-grenade, and understood him to say that the rearguard had them. I approached the rearguard – a few men holding the lane entrance, lit up by the burning buildings. When I asked one of them where I would find a hand-grenade, he pointed to the burning Post Office and said, 'In there.'

O'Rahilly was shouting, 'Are you Irishmen, that you won't charge?' and some men stepped forward more promptly. Bayonets were not numerous amongst us, but I noticed one man who stepped forward for the charge; he was armed with a shotgun and a bayonet made of 1" x 3/16" Bessemer steel, which had been made in Kimmage. A number of these bayonets had been made in Kimmage, but they would have bent against three-ply wood. O'Rahilly had got his party.

I did not notice which way they went, but apparently they went around Henry Street and charged down Moore Street. I heard the burst of fire, then the sound of running feet, then the sound of one man's feet, then silence.

By this time, the firing from the white house had ceased, and Mick Collins was improvising a barricade of barrels across a critical point, across a street down which the British were firing. Connolly was now carried by, in relative safety. Another Volunteer and myself took up our wounded man and followed.

As machine-gun fire from the enemy positions in the Rotunda Hospital and down Moore Lane increased, it was critical to gain cover. By this time, we had about eighteen to twenty wounded. Volunteers were breaking into houses. I heard one of them shout, 'Stand Clear!' and then burst the lock of one door with a shot or shots. Unfortunately, a girl and her father were trying to open the door. Both were hit, she fatally.

Sean MacDermott, limping quickly forward into the house with the men, was asking, 'Who has done this?' As MacDermott repeated this question, very intensely, the woman of the house herself was insisting that it was an accident and the Volunteers were not to be blamed.

Connolly was taken into this small house, and was being carried upstairs on his stretcher. I gave a hand on the narrow staircase, so narrow that Connolly was sometimes almost perpendicular. It was impossible to take him up these stairs until four of us lifted him horizontally, at extended arms length, over the banister-rail. While this was being done, the stretcher was sometimes at an acute angle – but James Connolly made no attempt to clutch the sides of his stretcher. He remained calm, though he was obviously in extreme pain, and remarked, 'A heavy load, chum,' recognising my London accent.

Nearly all of our wounded had been carried into that first house. We were considerably compressed, for a time, having not yet broken through into other buildings. The press was extreme until some men broke through the walls and extended. The men were so exhausted and disoriented that this technique of extension – in which we were all trained and by now quite experienced – did not begin until one of the daughters of the house suggested it to us.

We all knew that our position was now very vulnerable. Some of the wounded men were asking for water. Some men gave it willingly, but had to be asked. It is strange how soon one can get accustomed to another's pain. They were probably all thirsty – a thing I was not subject to. I remember hearing James Connolly mention quietly how he would 'dearly love a cup of tea'. However, we did what we could for the wounded. Ever afterwards, whenever I got the smell of chloroform or cordite, I would associate it with that room.

In the adjoining house, where the father and daughter were shot, a woman was crying, 'My child! Oh, my child!' I looked around for the child, thinking of an infant, and saw on the ground a piece of skull, about the size of a half orange; it was clean, and white, as I imagined a baby's would be. I slipped it into my mac pocket so that no one would discover it.

There was a Red Cross man with me when we entered that house. The father lay near the window on a bed. He had been wounded in the chest, and his wound had been dressed. His daughter, not quite yet a young woman, was lying on another bed – lifeless. I put my hand on her arm – the body was quite warm – and declared, 'She's alive!'

The Red Cross man said, 'No,' and showed me the broken skull – a piece of which I had in my pocket. I was still unconvinced until our one and only medical student saw her again and said what I still did not believe – that she really was dead.

The poor girl's father was without bitterness. Sean Mac-Dermott again offered to carry out an inquiry in the family's presence if the man thought that the Volunteers were guilty of brutality or negligence; but both parents were insistent that no one was to blame. By a tragic irony, that family had been sympathetic to the Volunteers' cause, and continued to show this; the mother cooked a very large quantity of potatoes, which was all the food she had. She was trying to improvise some sort of breakfast for our men on the following morning.

'COMRADE' AGAIN – THE DARKEST HOUR

I put on a Red Cross armlet in that house. There was some thought that it might be efficacious; certainly it gave me more liberty of movement. I had left a man apparently dying on the top floor of the next house. I had been busy, but went back to have a look at him. He was lying on the floor, badly wounded in the abdomen – a haversack of shotgun cartridges he had been carrying was hit and had exploded. The Red Cross man and I trussed him like a chicken to compress the stomach; he had bled an awful lot. I put my long mac under him. It was only then that I recognised him. It was 'Comrade'.

Two of our officers were sleeping on a bed in an adjoining room. One was a poet. He should have known better. We took their mattress. One takes what one will in a revolution – and 'Comrade' got the benefit of it.

I saw him every now and again. He was still feeling cold, and I pretended to pile more things on him. He always asked very brightly, 'How are things going, Comrade?' and, at last, consoled me by saying, 'The darkest hour is before the dawn.'

It would be a long time yet before the dawn.

As far as possible, no lights, or very few, were lighted. Fires for cooking were used with great discretion, because any smoke from them drew snipers' fire. The Volunteers were worn out. Most of them lay in any position. Some food had been brought from the Post Office. Pearse had insisted that every man carry provisions. One or two tried to cook rashers and tea – with little success. Mick Collins was one of these. He would listen to no one, but fastidiously cut himself bacon, cleaned a very dirty pan, and placed it on a small fire. He was warned not to put on more fuel, but persisted. Then a sniper hit the chimney, and his pan was full of soot. Mick was absolutely furious – and his language was choice.

Most of the Volunteers, it seemed, had rosaries, which they used more often as the situation became worse. I was sitting at the top of a staircase, my head drooping. Mick saw me and said, 'Are you ... praying, too?'

'You're in a sweet mood,' I replied, and followed him to the street door.

Some Volunteers had built a barricade, and had been there all night. They asked Mick what he thought of it – that barricade. What he said was uncomplimentary: '... your *barricade*!!' Poor Mick; he had more knowledge – of what had happened and would happen – and had had more hopes of what might have happened, and he had a far greater disappointment than any of us. But I did not know that then.

Most of the men by this time were utterly exhausted and apparently despondent. A large number in the more or less darkened rooms were saying their rosaries. During this period, I noticed one other group of young men. I had heard some talk of their being part of a bayonet-charge that was impending. And these young men I found discussing the hereafter somewhat academically. Others slept.

Suddenly, sometime in the middle of the night, everyone was awakened by a massive explosion. The fire – or maybe a stray shell – had at last reached the depths of the GPO basement, and our arsenal of abandoned dynamite and other explosives had obviously gone up. Shockwaves travelled through our little crowded houses.

★ ★ ★

After the Volunteers had bored through the buildings, our headquarters staff – Pearse, Plunkett and James Connolly, but not Tom Clarke – were passing the night in one room. James Connolly, lying on a bed, was conscious the whole time in that room – through which men passed to and fro. The room was barely twelve feet square – the sleeping apartment of a poor family. An oleograph of the Sacred Heart was on one wall, and on another wall one of Robert Emmett.

Whenever I saw Connolly, he appeared to be chatting quietly with the others. In that same room, there was a wounded British soldier, a Dublin Fusilier, who was injured badly in the groin. He was delirious, and was calling on Connolly – that is to say, he said: 'Jim Connolly ... Jim Connolly', many times. Padraig Pearse went to him at least once, and stayed talking with this wounded man for some time. At other times he would move from house to house, talking gently with our own men. He would then return and sit again with Joe Plunkett at the edge of Connolly's bed. That this private British soldier was cared for in the same room as our own headquarters staff was somehow typical of the style and calibre of our leaders.

The soldier moaned a great deal. It's worth mention, perhaps, that he wouldn't have been there if our captain, George Plunkett, hadn't gone out into Moore Street in a hail of British bullets to rescue him. George had then returned to salvage that soldier's rifle and ammunition, again under heavy fire.

We still had two of our nurses with us, two young girls of the Cumann na mBan, and, of course, Connolly's secretary, Miss Kearney, who had worked in close association with James Connolly for years. On our retreat from the Post Office, I'd had a glimpse of her, bending over his stretcher, shielding his body from bullets as he'd been carried across Henry Street. She was constantly by his side: plain, strong, determined, brusque – like himself. It was a kind of marriage.

I don't think the leaders had any food, except for some biscuits and some cups of tea, the water for which I got from some of the Volunteers. Water was hard to procure, at least in my vicinity, because, though there was a tap in the yard, one ran the danger of being sniped at in attempting to get there.

During this time, another man named O'Carroll and myself gave all the assistance we could to the wounded. Sean MacDermott had once more talked to the civilian who had been wounded – still very concerned that we had been responsible for the death of his daughter and for his own wounding. But the man said he was quite satisfied that it had been an accident; that he was opening the door when the Volunteers were trying to gain entry into the house.

The sounds of gunfire and artillery continued to be heard from many directions. With the exception of one man, there appeared to be no aggressive leadership. This was a young man, Sean McLoughlin, who was dressed in a Fianna Boys[24] uniform. I would say that he was about twenty-one years of age, but looked much younger, though not younger than many. He came and spoke frequently to our headquarters staff. At one time he was proposing a plan to them whereby he could release the stores out of a nearby shop. These stores consisted of turpentine, linseed oil and other inflammable or combustible liquids. He planned to release these liquids across the pavement and into the street,

---

24 Republican youth movement emphasising physical and military training.

to ignite them if and when the wind was favourable, and to charge through the fire at the military barricade at the top of Moore Street.

Another plan, suggested by a fiery Corkman, J.J. Walsh, was that we return to the ruins of the GPO, the walls of which still stood, though the interior was burned out. Both men also suggested that we attempt to link up with our lads who were, we believed, still holding out at the Four Courts. A charge against the British barricade could be a diversion to cover our main body's retreat. But, I wondered then – and still do – 'retreat where'? Perhaps both of these plans were impracticable, but those who proposed them would have attempted them. They had initiative and daring, and obviously believed in the maxim that a plan, even a bad plan, is better than no plan.

It seemed to me that our leaders were deliberating on all this, because Sean McLoughlin came back on several occasions asking for their consent. I noticed then that McLoughlin wore yellow stripes on his tunic shirt. I had the impression that they were the insignia of James Connolly's Citizen Army. When I'd first seen McLoughlin, he had no such stripes, but on the second occasion I saw him he was wearing them. They were of good quality, and obviously only recently attached. Every time he entered, he freely discussed his plans with the members of the staff, and seemed to have authority by their collective consent.

INSIDE THE GPO

Joe Plunkett still sat at the foot of Connolly's bed. Everyone was dead beat, including the women.

WITH GHQ IN MOORE STREET – SATURDAY, 29 APRIL

In the early hours of Saturday morning, work began again on extending our positions in the row of small buildings. Burrowing and tunnelling was completed through our small houses down the north side of Moore Street. We had moved our headquarters party, with great difficulty (especially for James Connolly), to a more central position. Young Sean McLoughlin had by this time found his twenty or so volunteers for the still-impending charge against the British barricade. Rifle and artillery fire had resumed, and could be heard from distant and nearby places.

Sometime later that morning, a party of civilians, mostly women, were attempting to leave from the other side of Moore Street. We received an order to cease fire, and this order was obeyed, though there was still considerable firing from enemy positions. I thought that the British had agreed in some way to the evacuation of women. Some men among the civilians had been warned not to go, but they persisted. I heard this order shouted by the enemy: 'Females advance and males stand.' Then there was a burst of fire. The women had managed to cross the street. But one man, at least, was riddled with bullets. He lay there on a white sheet, attached to a sweeping brush.

BEFORE THE SURRENDER –
WITH PEARSE AND CONNOLLY, 29 APRIL

It was that incident, perhaps, more than any other – and
the increasing possibility of others like it – which determined Pearse and his staff to treat for terms with the enemy.
Orders had been passed along to 'Hold your fire' to all of
our positions. Soon after that, I heard MacDermott calling
out, 'Does anyone around here have something we can use
for a white flag?'

Later again, I saw one of the girls – it was Elizabeth Fitzgerald[25] – with what seemed to be no more than a white hand-
kerchief tied to a piece of stick. She was led to a doorway
by MacDermott and one of our officers. There was at first
a burst of sustained firing as the improvised flag was waved
from the doorway. Then, there was silence. The girl stepped
into the street. She was a very pretty girl, and very pale. Many
of the Volunteers could see her go, walking very slowly up
Moore Street, alone, towards the British barricades.

It seemed a very long time before she was to return.

Connolly, Pearse and Plunkett were talking quietly and
occasionally laughing, like men who had made a decision
and were passing the time. I was told to bring Tom Clarke. I
said I did not know him. I'd meant something different, that
I had not personally met him, but that I knew very well who

---

25 Elizabeth O'Farrell.

he was, and what he was, and would have *liked* very much to know him. They laughed together, very good-humouredly. 'Not know Tom Clarke!' one of them said.

I went and found Tom. He was standing near a window, silent and alone. A quiet, gentle little man, there was nothing in his appearance to suggest that he was an old Fenian of the earlier generation. And yet, he was the Revolution.

Our young woman had come back, and then returned again to the British, bearing further messages. On her return to us the second time, she brought with her the terms of surrender. I did not hear the conversations that followed, but I knew that our leaders were discussing surrender, as I heard enough of the British note, which was read out openly, to know what terms were being sought.

Pearse had asked for no terms for himself, but only for the men who had fought under him. There was one British demand that stated that Connolly must be handed over at once. On Elizabeth Fitzgerald's *[sic]* third journey to the British position, P.H. Pearse accompanied her. I did not see them go. Padraig Pearse had, apparently, agreed to surrender himself unconditionally.

Sean McLoughlin was still in that room, and demurred strongly when he heard of the terms. He was insisting that the honours of war be given us. I do not know whether this was incorporated in our replies to the British, but it occurred to me afterwards that it probably must have been – and showed great foresight on Sean McLoughlin's part, because we might have left Moore Street, as would our other garrisons throughout Dublin, with our hands above our heads instead of, as we eventually did, in military formation and carrying our arms. The British might have treated us much more ignominiously. So I have always thought that this condition must have been accepted.

Connolly now sat up in bed and shaved himself. It must have been an ordeal, considering his wounds, which were grave, both physical and mental. Yet he was cheerful. Miss Kearney held the looking glass for him, sitting somewhat awkwardly by his side on the bed. She was leaning across his body as he shaved himself with a cut-throat razor.

Joe Plunkett was sitting at the end of the bed. He had lost one of his spurs. I pointed this out to him, sensitive for his dignity when he would face the enemy. He must have known what was in my mind, and said, smiling, 'The doctors give me six months to live.' He took the other spur off and kicked it with a quiet tap under Connolly's bed.

When Connolly finished shaving, Miss Kearney turned to me and said, 'This is bad. It will break his heart. He has worked hard for this all his life.' Then she added, turning to Connolly, 'The Kimmage lads — what will happen to them?' He replied quietly to her — I did not hear what he said.

I mentioned to Joe Plunkett that some of us might have acquired things or property not our own during that week, and I suggested that he authorise me to tell the men to leave behind them things of value that they might have acquired, lest it be thought we had been looting. I'd encountered one of our lads who was secreting an expensive watch – it was his own property – in an old grandfather clock. He was hopeful of coming back later to collect his watch. I felt less sanguine of my own return anywhere at that moment.

At some time before Connolly left our building, I was sent to find a barber. I was unable to locate one. But Winifred Kearney and Julia Grenan[26], the only other young woman still with us, had combed his hair, washed him, redressed his wounds, and were making his stained, dusty uniform as presentable as was possible.

Four very smart men in uniform arrived. Connolly was taken from the room by these four Volunteers. They were washed, shaved and polished as if for a parade. The insurrection was over. I shall never see such noble and simple men again.

---

26 Sheila Grennan.

THE SURRENDER

WHEN SOME OF the men were told of the surrender, they were furious, especially our London, Liverpool, Manchester and Glasgow men – the hardcore of the Kimmage garrison. I agreed with the contention that the Kimmage garrison itself would come off badly. It was argued that we, the Kimmage lads, had nothing to lose, and that we might as well fight to the end. During this last period in Moore Street, I had heard only one man mention surrender, but he was wounded. He'd spoken of it dispassionately, as if it would occur to any fool. And one group I came across – who favoured fighting on – were discussing the hereafter matter-of-factly. They didn't care if fighting on meant being wiped out. These were very young home-born Irishmen. It was not a pose. They were all close friends.

The situation was serious, bordering on something close to mutiny, though up to this time all the men had followed orders and accepted discipline from their officers as if they'd been hardened troops of many years' experience.

This anger and argument among our British-born contingent was becoming critical. They believed that if they surrendered they would all be treated as deserters, most of them having English accents. They said that if they were in danger of being shot as deserters, they would prefer to be killed still fighting the British army. Many others believed they would be conscripted if captured, and anything was preferable to that. I was sympathetic; I had an English accent myself, and believed with them that our position was the least enviable of any who surrendered. The fact that we were all sure that our leaders would be shot or hanged made it seem very likely that the enemy would execute many of us in a general sweep.

During the seemingly unending wait for the final terms of surrender, things were moving swiftly towards a decision to fight on, especially among the Kimmage garrison. Worse, our hot-tempered desperation was beginning to arouse a response from the Volunteers as a whole, and also from the few Citizen Army men who remained – tough nuts who would balk at nothing, whatever the consequences. The men were not despairing – as might have been imagined by our enemy – but had become more militant since Pearse and Connolly had gone. Pearse, as our Commander-in-Chief, who had been designated first President of the proclaimed Republic, had been a father-figure, and he had proved himself worthy of the title of a true leader. But if Pearse was the soul of the Rising, James Connolly was its heart. And though he too had just been taken from us, the heart of this revolution was still beating.

If the men had their way, we were heading for slaughter. Something had to be done to stop them. Four very different men were to try, but it didn't seem possible to me then that any one of them had any chance of succeeding.

Old Tom Clarke was the first to try. He wasn't very old[27] – just tired and spent. He did his best to persuade us, and I was impressed by his eloquence. He insisted that only himself and the other leaders would be shot by the British. He mentioned his fifteen years in English jails for his Fenian activities. He told us that there was no need for us to fight to the death; that we had done well already. He said he was confident that, as a result of our action, the Irish people would now assert themselves. Because of us, he claimed, 'Ireland's future has now been secured.'

He spoke at length, and with great force and sincerity, and said many other things I greatly wish I could now remember, but he failed to convince anyone. And Mick Collins failed just as completely, which surprised me. He was tough, even belligerently so, challenging us with the argument that if we fought on it would mean we'd achieve nothing but the absolutely certain death-warrants of *all* our leaders. Some

---

27 Clarke was fifty-nine.

man interjected that 'They'll all be shot anyway!' However, I now believe Mick was thinking of something else; of the future importance of our junior officers, and not because he was one such himself, but he was – with his typical intelligence and foresight – already organising the next phase of our resistance. But on this occasion Mick had no success. He was at his very best always in dealing with one or a few individuals. He was never a great hand with a crowd, though that skill came much later in his life. Perhaps too late.

Even poor Joe Plunkett, already at the point of death, dragging himself to us and pleading with that austere, stoic passion, could not move us. Joseph Mary Plunkett, with a talent for words, the maker of such luminous poems, leader of men into impossible battles, could not dissuade us from this certain last one. I was becoming thoroughly alarmed – more so I think than I had been since I'd stood on O'Connell Bridge that previous Monday. Thank God for MacDermott, who was to save our dignity, and maybe our necks.

Sean MacDermott was the mind of the revolution. And if those others of our remarkable leaders were its body and soul, he showed us often that he was its head. He limped forward briskly, leaning on that light cane, taking great care to call us all together into one group. The recalcitrants had divided repeatedly into several arguing sections. MacDermott released his astonishing wide smile, cobalt-blue eyes shining into every face.

'Now, what exactly is it,' said he, leaning easy on his cane like any civil servant in his still entirely civilian suit, 'that you all want to do?'

There was a silence. And then he was assailed with all of the arguments. He listened, very, very carefully, with a sort of charmed concentration. When everyone had finished, there was another short silence. And then he began to speak, very quietly, with enormous concentration. And total confidence. His was the most powerful personality I'd ever encountered. I don't know if he was a Marxist – he was, as many of us knew, Tom Clarke's protege – but it was the sheer scale of his persona that mattered. Politics at its best is the art of knowing women and men. I was told much later, and could believe it, that most women loved him. It was his eyes that did everything. Yet the words were simple enough.

He suggested that we take a long look at the dead civilians lying in the street outside our windows. He asked us to imagine how many more of them would be lying there if we fought on. He also stressed that the civilians nearest us were all very poor, and would be butchered with us. He said that the rest of 'this beautiful city' would be razed. 'You've all seen what happened to the Post Office!' He told us that the worst that would happen to the Irish Volunteers from England would be 'a few years' in jail. He said we'd 'fought a gallant fight', and we'd only lose now by fighting further. He told us that our only remaining duty now was to survive.

He used the word 'survive', I remember, several times: 'The thing that you must do, all of you, is to survive!' He ended by insisting quietly, and still smiling, that 'We, who will be shot, will die happy – knowing that there are still plenty of you around who will finish the job.'

I had heard quite a number of speeches during that week, and the earlier ones were impressive, but that quiet speech was the most potent that I was privileged to hear.

The insurrection was over. Its aftermath was already beginning. Collins and others who survived would see to it that the deeds, as well as the words, of that week would not be wasted.

LAST IMAGES – JOE PLUNKETT AND THE O'RAHILLY

One man stood in that deserted street, alone, except for the dead. Joe Plunkett, tall and elegant, stood in the middle of Moore Street, holding a white flag, his back turned to the enemy. About one hundred yards distant was the British military barricade, crowded with soldiers and guns. Some houses further away were also crowded with military. I was fascinated by the unconscious staging. The British troops were all curiosity, staring at his back. He was unaware of the effect of his attitude, which looked scornful. For him the enemy did not appear to exist. It was as if the white flag had enshrouded his soul.

British snipers were still firing at us, making it difficult to evacuate our wounded. Joe Plunkett saw me watching him from the doorway and beckoned me to him. I went out on the road to him. He was still alone on the street. Joe sent me to the barricade to inform the British military of our difficulty.

As I walked to the barricade, there was absolute silence. Even soldiers can feel awed, it would appear. I halted about four feet from the barricade, in continued silence. It was a robust affair, made of railway sleepers, which were to assume much significance to me later, although I did not realise that then.

When I reached the barricade, I looked at an officer who had clambered up on it, but did not speak until he crossed over the barricade to me. Then I saluted. He returned my salute. He waited for me to speak, but I remained silent until he addressed me himself. Taking some care to diminish my London accent, I then delivered my message; he gave me an answer, and I returned to Joe in absolute silence.

Our wounded were brought out into Moore Street and left on the footpath. I did not know what arrangements, if any, were made for them. I asked Joe Plunkett, and he sent me back again up to the barricade to ask the officer what provision would be made for our wounded.

The officer replied that he had no orders in this matter, but shouted that he would be moving into the street with his men, and was very irate and discourteous, giving me a deadline. To quicken his interest, I said, 'A number of yours, your own wounded, are amongst ours.' He then foolishly asked me who had shot them. I don't know if I smiled. That officer was not smiling, but there was a dead cat lying in the road that might have been.

As I returned I noticed The O'Rahilly. He was lying at the corner of a laneway, his head in the direction of the British barricade. He had got very near to it. He looked handsome, even in death. I noticed his waxed moustache. There were no obvious signs of his wounds. I would have liked to take a memento of him for his family – perhaps only a button – but time did not permit.

The Volunteers were forming up in the street. A number of the dead were lying around: civilians, soldiers and Volunteers. One of the civilian casualties was squatting against a wall with a white bundle; his head was slit open like a pomegranate. A Volunteer was lying at the corner of Moore Lane, a dead Tommy beside him. I'll never forget that little Volunteer. I looked at him. He was very dead. They had played a machine-gun on him. Pieces of wool, his undergarments, protruded through his uniform, making a scarecrow character of a man I was once very fond of. It was Paddy Shortiss[28], one of the first to step out for that bayonet charge. I knelt and covered his staring eyes with a soldier's haversack and

---

28 Originally from Ballybunion, County Kerry.

said the shortest of prayers. A small cheer came from the Volunteer ranks – don't know why.

One of our own officers – I don't remember who – was reading out the last orders from Pearse, the note of surrender. Those few words are well known and have been documented. It might be fitting that they could be quoted in these pages; the last words written by Pearse – or Connolly. They might stand here, at this juncture. Just as the Proclamation had ushered in the Rising, these few words had ended it. The Proclamation of the Republic, written by Padraig Pearse, would stand among any in the world, for its style as much as its aspirations; and these words, which he had now chosen to end our battle, have the same nobility. It's fitting that they can now be found in any Irish child's history book.

In order to prevent the further slaughter of Dublin citizens, and in the hope of saving the lives of our followers now surrounded and hopelessly outnumbered, the members of the Provisional Government present at Headquarters have agreed to an unconditional surrender, and the Commandants of the various districts in the City and Country will order their commands to lay down arms.

P.H. Pearse

29th April 1916

3:45 P.M.

I agree to these conditions for the men only under my own command in the Moore Street District and for the men in the Stephen's Green Command.

James Connolly

April 29/16

Our Fianna lad, Sean McLoughlin, called the Volunteers to attention in Moore Street, and proceeded to read the short note which referred to the exact details of our surrender: 'Carrying a white flag, proceed down Moore Street, turn into Moore Lane and Henry Place, out into Henry Street, and around the Pillar to the right hand side of O'Connell Street, march up to within a hundred yards of the military drawn up at the Parnell statue, halt, advance five paces and lay down arms.'

McLoughlin concluded his address to the men by saying, 'The officers will fall-in at the rear.' Which they did. Then he said, 'The men will be allowed to proceed home.' There was a small cheer; but Sean corrected what he had read and said, 'The men will lay down their arms in O'Connell Street.' I've often wondered about that mistake, or – perhaps – seeming mistake. That mere boy, who had, perhaps more than anyone, secured us such honourable and dignified ritual, had enough nerve to chance any trick that might release any men to seed the future confrontation with an enemy who now thought that they had defeated us. I also remember that Sean most carefully ordered that our varied armaments, including the odd rifle magazine, be carefully unloaded.

I had a word with 'Comrade' before I left. We said we would meet again. We never did. Some kindhearted Tommy loosened his bindings and he died in three hours, I was told later.

We marched out by the same route by which we had fought our way in: by Moore Lane, Henry Place, Henry Street, and past the Post Office. Above it, one of our flags – the tricolour – was still flying. The whole length of O'Connell Street was a wreck. It occurred to me that someone would be made to pay for this. The Volunteers were drawn up in a line from the front of Findlater's, extending back to about the Gresham Hotel. I arrived at the rear of our party, since I'd stayed behind to speak to the wounded. I would say that in all, there were about 120 of us there. Our men had just stepped forward to deposit their arms. We were drawn up in single file, each one of us covered by a soldier behind us with fixed bayonet. The atmosphere was very tense – as though they would butcher us at the least provocation.

Some of the junior British officers stepped forward and began to meddle with and inspect the arms we had deposited. I considered this rather undisciplined, not to say dangerous – any one of those weapons might have exploded – and I was holding my breath. It was still very quiet. There seemed to be much surprise at the smallness of our numbers.

Major General[29] Lowe was present. He passed along the ranks of the Volunteers and addressed me, saying, 'What is *your* name?'

I answered, somewhat flippantly, 'Good.' He apparently thought that this was a joke. I noticed his indignation and added, 'G-o-o-d, Good,' whereupon he said, 'Come on, you're not dead yet!' I answered this by saying, 'No bloody fear, I'm not.'

He then attempted to strike me with his riding-cane across the legs, and I jumped in the air, missing the cane; whereupon there was a scream of inane laughter from some British officers who were standing at the entrance to the Gresham Hotel. Lowe then completely lost his head and shouted, 'Go in, the whole bloody lot of you!'

They fled like sheep, scrambling through the doorway behind them. I was to hear later that he was caught napping by the Germans and shot in his pyjamas. I liked the bit about the pyjamas – it took the bad taste out of my mouth.[30]

---

29 At this time, Brigadier.

30 There was a General Loder, father of a young officer who later became a British film actor (John Loder), who actually received Pearse's sword. John Loder died in Hollywood quite recently, a little-known actor, almost forgotten; but the presence of his father and of himself on that historic occasion at the end of Moore Street was mentioned in his obituary. There is a photograph of Loder, his father and Pearse, which has an odd, dignified pathos. Pearse was a reasonably 'fine figure of a man', but appears curiously nondescript here, shrunk, bedraggled, diminished by battle, despite that slouched hat with its panache affected by so many of his men.

It would, perhaps, only be fair to say how some of the harsh treatment we received from some of our enemy arose. The bearing and behaviour of the Volunteers was that of men who had done something laudable and, as their behaviour had been chivalrous, they expected that military etiquette would be observed by the enemy. The British soldiers, officers and men, were obviously irritated and puzzled by the Volunteers. They were shocked at the small numbers that had surrendered, and at the variety and crudity of our arms. They all regarded the Volunteers as shameless, impertinent traitors, and said so.

The following incident illustrates this. One British sergeant was very indignant, and said, 'Look at this that you fired!' as he put something under the nose of a youthful Volunteer. He was holding up for inspection a 'Howth' rifle bullet. It was soft-nosed, fully an inch in diameter, wedged in the cartridge case with paper, a bullet as large as one's thumb – big enough to kill an elephant. 'A bloody "dum-dum"!' said the outraged sergeant.

The boy replied with a sob in his voice at this imputation, 'Well, you wouldn't let us get the right stuff!' Some of the Volunteers laughed aloud.

A column of Volunteers was approaching on the opposite side of O'Connell Street, marching briskly from the direction of O'Connell Bridge. They were halted just in front of us. Someone said, 'Ah, now there are Daly's men!'[31] We

---

31 The Four Courts garrison.

were still standing with bayonets nearly touching our backs, while Daly's men came to surrender with cigarettes and cigars lighted, as if out for a holiday. The column was by now halted, but the men still smoked. Orders were shouted by the military to 'Stop smoking!' They were an incorrigible bunch – most of them continued smoking. Then came an order in an unmistakable Etonian accent, 'Stop that smoking.' Some wag in the Daly ranks repeated the order – and accent – with perfect cadence, and this was followed by a peal of laughter from the other side of the street. The bayonet at my back suppressed my inclination to laugh, but I felt I'd have liked to know Daly, who could do this with men. Even when they had deposited their arms, they continued to smoke. Apparently, at this stage these Volunteers would take orders only from their own officers.

Some of the British officers were still making scathing remarks about our heterogeneous collection of arms. This was very painful to some Volunteers, working men who had sacrificed hard-earned shillings to purchase their own equipment, though it was true that some of those rifles dated from the period of Garibaldi.

We were then all marched and herded on to the small patch of grass in front of the Rotunda Hospital, and forced back until we were closely packed. There was barely standing room. We were surrounded by bayonets, and we gradually sank down and squatted somehow. Those nearest the margin of the grass plot were threatened with rifle butts when they attempted to stretch their feet out on the pathway.

One wretched little British officer flashed a lamp in our faces, saying, 'I know this one – and that one ...!' He had been our prisoner in the GPO, and had been decently treated. 'Ape-Face', 'Pig-face', 'Beast-Face' were just some of the expressions he used. He made some remark about my particular friend, Garret MacAuliffe, and Garret replied, '*You* are no bloody Adonis!' That put a stop to the annoyance for a time. But it was the same officer who later made unpleasant remarks on Sean MacDermott's lameness, and then grabbed Sean's walking-cane away from him. Another officer, an Irishman who was later a detective for British intelligence, was even more offensive and brutal, stripping some of our men. I distinctly heard a comment from Mick Collins to pass the word, 'We'll get that fellow's name.' Four years later, I believe, 'that fellow' – then an inspector of RIC intelligence – came to a violent and sudden end.[32]

SUNDAY, 30 APRIL

We remained at the Rotunda for about twelve hours. It was very uncomfortable in many ways, and seemed a very long night. We'd been so closely packed, it was impossible

---

32 Captain Lee Wilson, later an RIC district inspector in Gorey, County Wexford, was killed in June 1920. Collins, according to Joe, 'always finished a job'.

to relieve ourselves in any way until the morning. When we were allowed to rise to our feet, at last, a cloud of steam arose. When we had got to our feet, the hospital windows of the Rotunda were crowded with nurses looking down at us – another misgiving for me about the glories of war. But, as we marched through O'Connell Street a few minutes later, a lone Dublin fireman shouted out, 'God bless you, boys!' That was the first word of approval I had heard from Dubliners during that whole week. He had been hosing down the still-smoking ruins just before O'Connell Bridge. When I looked back at the front of our 'Kelly's Fort' on Bachelor's Walk, I could see that it was now merely a burned-out husk, with shell-holes gaping through the facade.

Sean MacDermott, some way behind and now without his cane, was limping along, supporting himself on the arms of two very young Volunteers.

It was a nice irony that we were being marched through the place of our St Patrick's Day parade, around College Green and up Dame Street. Women ran out of the side streets, screaming at us, and would have attacked us, no doubt, but for our British escorts. These men were conscripts. I said to the soldier marching beside me, 'It's a queer situation when a rifle is forced into your hand to take one out of mine.'

'It ain't my fault, mate,' he replied. No, it never was, poor little soldier.

As we passed through High Street, near St Audoen's Church, crowds of Dublin women were in the side streets, and they shouted, 'Bayonet them! Bayonet them!' Most of these women were poor 'shawlies' from the back streets; others were more well-to-do and as hostile. But they were kept back by the British soldiers.

We had reached Richmond Barracks – now Keogh Barracks – and stood in the broiling sun for hours, it seemed. Men began collapsing in the ranks. Had we been left there another half hour, few of us, I think, would have been left standing. One of the first to fall was Joe Plunkett. Two British soldiers lifted him by the shoulders and dragged him to the footpath.

I'm surprised more of us hadn't collapsed. We had been twenty hours without a drop of water. A party of British soldiers – Irishmen of an Irish Regiment, I think – rushed towards us, shouting, and would have attacked us had they not been halted by our guards. But since the surrender, the private soldiers and NCOs had behaved very correctly towards us. After a considerable number of Volunteers had collapsed, a soldier came along with a bucket of water. He reaped a rich harvest. Volunteers gave him anything they had, including personal belongings such as rings – in gratitude, perhaps – or thinking possessions of little further value. It struck me that our men gave their belongings partly because they thought they would have no further use for them. When I was being approached, I said, 'I have nothing to give you.' The bucket passed to a better customer. Somehow I never felt thirsty – perhaps as a result of my distaste for water.

Eventually we were marched into the gymnasium of Richmond Barracks. As we filed past, we were observed closely and individually by a number of Dublin police detectives. Our fingerprints were taken. Some Volunteers resisted this, and were threatened on their refusal, but they were tired beyond fear. Later, as we sat on the floor, the detectives walked amongst us, picking out their prey. These included our 'Skipper', George Plunkett, and his brother Jack, who were both placed among a group of selected victims. Joe Plunkett and MacDermott had already been taken away.

Later we were placed in dormitories. I was sharing Mick Collins' overcoat. The floor was hard. A British sergeant said to Collins, 'What has you here, Collins?' and Mick replied, 'England's difficulty.'

There was a pause, before the Sergeant repeated, '"England's difficulty ..." – and what the hell's that?'

Mick lightly completed the old adage: 'Well, England's difficulty is – Ireland's opportunity.'

A young fellow of our company – a very young boy – then asked, 'I wonder will they try to force us into the British army?'

I said out loud that 'They wouldn't touch us with a forty-foot pole.'

The sergeant, who was still listening, shouted out, 'Shut your bloody mouth!' But Mick squeezed my knee delightedly.

That night we were marched to the boat. Before our departure, we were given iron rations. We were served with tins of bully beef and some bread, a tin of bully to every two men. There was an uneven number in my group – so I was content to be last. But a sergeant standing by asked me, 'What regiment was it *you've* deserted from?'

My accent could get me into trouble, but this too had its rewards. A young soldier came back amongst my group with some steaming mugs of tea, and said to me, '*I'm* not against you, mate.'

We were soon marching to the boat that would take us to England. We halted at O'Connell Bridge. There was no avoiding that bridge, it seemed. I was with a group of Volunteer officers: Ned Morkan, Seamus Murphy, Harry Nicholls, W.M. O'Reilly and some others. Our company officers compared very favourably with any British officers I had seen. They were not at all disheartened.

O'Connell Street was a pile of smoking ruins. Our military escorts relieved themselves against a shattered and now steaming wall. I felt it was the last indignity. I was bitter and sore and felt ridiculous. I said to a Volunteer officer beside me, Ned Morkan, 'We are the last of the Mohicans – hundreds of years too late.'

'Don't be cynical, Joe,' said Ned. 'If they let you live six months, you will be amazed at the change. You will see the reaction.' He meant that the Irish people, and Dubliners especially, would change their attitude to the Easter Rising – and he was certainly right about that. But I did not have to wait for six months.

INTERNMENT

THE SHIP WHICH we boarded was near Liberty Hall. It was a cattle-boat, and we were taken down into the hold. One Volunteer who had lost his nerve asked, 'Are we going to be shot?'

A British sergeant replied, 'No, mate! You're not going to be shot. You're going to be *'ung!'*

A more cheerful Volunteer suggested that the English could nicely solve themselves a problem by slapping a torpedo into our cattle-boat, and as easily claim we were hit by a German submarine. Perhaps he was right. In fact he was very right, as history can show, because the entire personnel of what was afterwards to become our GHQ were aboard that boat: that is to say, Mick Collins, Dick Mulcahy, Gearoid O'Sullivan and others.

The journey to England was uneventful. When the boat arrived, our party was divided. Some were sent to Stafford, and the party I was with were sent to Knutsford Prison.

As we approached Knutsford Prison, there was only one hostile demonstrator, a clergyman who yapped and yapped and yapped at our heels. A Volunteer, a Liverpool docker, stepped out from our ranks and said a few words. The yapper fled. I've always wondered what it was that Liverpool docker said.

We were marched to our cells and slept and slept and slept. I think it was two days before I was aware of being awake. I ate what I was given, and fell asleep again. When I awoke I looked at my fairly comfortable bed, with sheets, pillow and blankets, and said to myself: 'Shades of John Mitchel – do they expect to break my heart with this?'

My bed was a gift, after a long week of action and some months of sleeping in a draughty mill on a bed of straw at Kimmage. Alas, they soon took the bed away, and I had to sleep again on hard planks. Other occupants of my cell, before my arrival there, had scratched their sentences and sentiments on the walls. One of these inscriptions was enigmatic: '60 days for an old soldier's crime! – roll on 25th!' I was curious about that inscription then, but not now. I don't want to know.

But there were other inscriptions to be placed upon those walls that would amaze future English prisoners. There was an outburst of poetry among the Volunteers – and almost all of it got written down. You could not get your poem heard unless you listened to the other fellow's drivel. I wrote my first – my first and last – poem on that wall. It was a young soldier's crime, I suppose, but it was no worse than those I was forced to hear from others.

We spent two months in Knutsford, at first in solitary confinement. Knutsford at that time was a military prison, and our warders were soldiers. With one exception, our keepers behaved correctly; but this man, a sergeant, was a sadist, and struck many Volunteers if they risked talking to each other.

After some weeks, we were allowed to go to mass. Our appearances were much altered. Our heads were cropped close, leaving a kind of Mahomet's tuft on the forehead. This was optional. I was completely bald, and was christened 'Death's Head'. The Volunteers bent their heads, after looking at their closest friends with suppressed, sobbing laughter. Our organist during the mass, one of our own lads, played 'Hail Glorious Saint Patrick' as we marched out from the chapel. When he'd come to the part 'Oh Come To Our Aid – Oh Come To Our Aid!' it was too much for those with a sense of humour.

It was not all fun in those lonely cells. Many had wives and children; others had parents or other relatives who did not know what had become of them. They expected the worst, because they believed the worst and had little knowledge of England and English politicians. Being a Londoner myself, and more familiar with the English than many, I felt a little less apprehensive about our ultimate fate. Or so I thought at the time, from what I considered the mature perspective of my twenty-odd years.

Meanwhile, we could not communicate with each other, and the only news we got was from the sentries: a whispered 'Another two of your blokes was shot this morning.' Not encouraging information for men many of whom still harboured thoughts or fears that they might be shot themselves. Our group at Knutsford Jail seemed to be considered something of the 'hardcore' of the insurrectionists; we had heard rumours that the main body of those interned were being held at the somewhat milder institution of Frongoch Camp in Wales.

This solitary confinement continued. There was nothing to read in our cells. That was hard enough for me, but it must have been agony to men of education, for some of our Volunteers, especially our younger officers, were well-read and articulate. Then, there was the constant gnawing of hunger. I have often wondered what prison officials put in the food that increases the pangs of hunger – probably a laxative, lest constipation ensue from the decreased activity.

For my part, I felt most the loss of the sky, and swore I would never complain but ever give thanks to God if I could see it in freedom once more. I knew the British, having brought us to England, would show restraint. There had been as yet no specific charges against me. And the war would end some day. I fully expected to get about seven years when they found out about my English birth, but I guessed that the main body of the men were too many to hold indefinitely. I had no family anxieties, and I was used to fending for myself. The members of my family had patience and common sense. But I pitied the others, and engaged the sentries outside my cell in conversations that might lead to information – any information I might then pass on. One sentry in particular, I thought, might be usefully corruptible, and I spoke to him continually through my spy-hole. I promised him things. He told me in a voice of awe that most of the others were praying. Our keepers were not too accustomed to men who prayed, it seemed.

Those warders and sentries put an especially high value on rosaries. They begged us for them. I thought it must be the superstition of men likely to go into action on the western front. I knew it was not piety. But it was neither. 'Rebel rosaries', it seemed, brought a high price in Manchester from Irish Catholics. This new nugget of information gave me solace. Perhaps this taste for rebel artifacts was as much a nationalist as a religious appetite. But hunger was my obsession. One waited for that distant rattle of cans proclaiming dinner, with an ear constantly at the cell door.

After six weeks or so, there was a sudden change in the treatment we received. We were allowed to smoke, receive parcels and even speak freely to each other. It seemed obvious to me that our jailers had been instructed to treat us more gently. Perhaps this was partly the result of the tactics of the prisoners themselves; tactics peculiar, apparently, to Irish prisoners or Irishmen – for when they were given an inch they took the proverbial mile.

Then, at last, one got a view of that prison from the idiotic exercise-ring. It was made of good red brick. Millions of bricks, up to four stories high and a wall all around; unscaleable, with a wall also of bricks enclosing that 'dome' of Oscar Wilde's sky;[33] millions of bricks, and each one of them seemed to have a personal grin. The architect had achieved his purpose perfectly. From inside that high wall, a prisoner was ever conscious of his captivity. And inside the prison, there was constant surveillance; one jailer standing in the hall could survey every corner.

There were flowers and a garden around the governor's house, but it was cut off by the high wall. Within that high wall was our circle of paving stones. We marched round this, three paces apart, and woe betide you if you were seen speaking to another prisoner.

Yet we were not wholly suppressed. One sentry was unreasonably officious, and I tried to revenge myself on him. As I passed I muttered, 'There was a little man', and when I passed him next time added, 'and he had a little gun!' I was reported

---

33 The allusion is to the prisoners' exercise yard in Oscar Wilde's 'Ballad of Reading Gaol', a favourite poem of my father's throughout his life.

for talking and cautioned. The governor was a decent fellow. I said that I was unconsciously quoting a nursery rhyme. He told me that this was a military prison, and no place for nursery rhymes. Perhaps he would have winked at me – but he had only one eye.

One day I got a shock, and found something I had lost as a child in London. Or, perhaps, began to find something again that I had never known I'd previously possessed or yearned for.

We were all marching around that idiotic circle of paving stones. A door opened in that high wall and I got a view of flowers in bloom and girls in pretty summer dresses. These were the first of our visitors, and my eyes were wet.

That evening I was brought from my cell and taken to what appeared to be the guardroom. Two handsome Highlanders with full kit were standing there. 'My escort,' I thought, 'come to take me to my trial.' I wished I was somewhat taller.

A sergeant said, 'Sign this,' pointing to an open book. I declined, saying I wouldn't sign anything until I had read it. He said, 'I don't give a damn if you do or not; the parcel is addressed to you.' Although I refused to sign, the parcel was thrust at me, and I was sent back to my cell, wondering.

When I was alone, I looked at the parcel a long time before at last opening it. It was addressed from a Miss Flynn of Manchester, and I did not know her from Eve – but blessings on her. The parcel contained large pork pies, the biggest and whitest of white loaves, and a huge slab of butter.

This was the first indication of what I had somehow expected. Perhaps the tide was turning at last. The blundering British had, they realised, gone too far in their treatment of us, and now would try the other tack. I divided my gift of grub into two parts, but still did not gorge, though greatly tempted. I guessed that more would be coming. In the morning my best friend, Garret MacAuliffe, stood at his open cell door, waiting as we all did for the order to empty our slops – a routine which started our days. I took a chance and ran down the balcony and threw his share of the grub at him. There was an agonised cry of 'Joe! – Go back! Go back!' Garret thought I had gone mad, knowing nothing of the conclusions I had drawn overnight from that sight of visitors – and that wonderful parcel.

My guess was justified. Within a couple of hours that day, we were free to talk, laugh and lounge in the sunshine at last, against those high brick walls. And the parcels were coming in. The tide *had* really turned; a people whose history is composed of personal loyalties were angry at a stranger hurting Mick, Peter or Patrick. From now on, at whatever the excuse, the Irish in England would badger the authorities on our behalf, just as the Irish at home and in America were now taking up our cause.

One woman from Manchester had picked my name by

chance. It was to be a delightful month. There were books to read and frequent visitors. I had to make the most of the books – expecting no visitors. And yet I had one visitor – a total stranger – and told this lady visitor to tell others to ask for me so I could get other visits.

I looked a terrible fright. My head was still cropped close, without even a 'Mahomet's tuft', and my beard was thick, curly and black, except where I had plucked the chin naked in solitary confinement. Tears came to those girls' eyes. I could only make them laugh in fits and starts. I spared their feelings by retiring early – but rewarded them for their parcels and tears. I told them that an Irish-born country lad was lonely for a caller, as he had no family connection in England. And soon enough 'handsome Joe Lawless' was requested by a visitor. He really was handsome. He had a picturesque wounded arm in a sling, and looked the true knight in his uniform and slouched hat. In gratitude, Joe insisted on giving me some old Irish pennies. Each of those pennies had an heroic history. I buttered the pennies up, literally, and burnished them brightly, before giving them as return gifts to lady visitors, who were delighted to have them.

Alfie Byrne, later to be a very long-time lord mayor of Dublin in the early years of the Irish Free State, came to Knutsford and distributed cigarettes. At first the Volunteers nearly attacked him, but something he said must have pacified them. At that time he was an MP, and told us something to the effect that he had condemned in parliament the executions of our leaders that were taking place in Ireland.

We were allowed to write letters at last, and although I still couldn't write home without risk of prejudicing someone's security, I was anxious to get a letter or so off to at least one or two more recent friends in the movement. Unfortunately, in the only letter I did write, I unwittingly contributed evidence as a result of which a man was given seven years. I'd written, hoping he was alive and well – it did not occur to me that a Volunteer could have escaped after the Rising – but my one letter was censored. His sister was not at all pleased to see me when I was released.

There was an aspect of that period in jail I have never been certain about. Some of the men were swearing that they would never, never surrender again. I echoed that resolution, with this difference: that I'd take good care to avoid the occasion of surrendering. I had been only three months in Ireland before the Easter Rising, and I had until then little acquaintance with native-born Irishmen. The Kimmage garrison were nearly all born and reared in England. I thought things over in my cell, and felt that I was not tough enough to be a comrade to native Irishmen.

I knew I had taken part in history, and I had satisfied the desire of my life. I had survived the fortunes of war without a scratch; and these young men were talking of the 'next time', and 'no more surrenders'. It was frightening.

Much of this heroic talk, I was to discover, was youthful posing and make-believe. The 'no surrender' mentality led us all later to disaster and fratricide. There were a few among us who would produce a 'next time' and a 'no surrender'. They were religious men who had found a vocation in the revolution. Their lives would end with a rope, a firing party or in a lunatic asylum. And these zealots would lead the mere talkers to condone acts that they – the talkers – secretly shivered at.

FRONGOCH INTERNMENT CAMP, NORTH WALES

It was already mid-summer when we were transferred to Frongoch Concentration Camp in north Wales. At first we were well-treated, given a surprising deal of liberty and sometimes taken on route marches. Frongoch, originally built for German prisoners of war in the Welsh hills, was relatively pleasant – after Knutsford – and it was very strange to have playing fields and comfortable army huts. We had our own cooks, and were subject to our own officers' discipline.

It had occurred to me, when we were being shipped from Dublin, that the British were allowing the most dangerous men to escape. These, our junior officers, were very obvious in their uniforms. They had all been elected by their own men after considerable winnowing, and they were the cream of the survivors among the Irish Volunteers. They compared favourably with professional British army officers;

their background and education were, if anything, superior to those of their English counterparts. They were to become financiers, barristers, engineers and industrialists, and achieve eminence in the first Irish Free State. These highly capable young men, who would normally have followed a profession or career, were anything but romanticists, and they were to become the headquarters staff of our active campaign from 1917 to 1921.

In Frongoch, the Volunteers clamoured to be recognised as 'prisoners of war'. Fortunately for us, the British government gave us the conditions of prisoners of war, even if they denied us the title. Professional British officers, who know a soldier when they see one, would have given the title, but demanded propriety and military discipline. And then the caste system of the British army would have decimated the Frongoch Volunteers, by driving a wedge between our officers and men.

As prisoners in Frongoch, we were originally divided into two sections: one section was housed in huts, the other section in a derelict old distillery. One of our officers, in his vanity, persisted in acting as an 'officer by the grace of God'. He inflicted pointless punishments, including incarceration in cells, and had a part of the camp entirely to himself. This officer had distinguished himself by fighting with great skill and bravery during the Rising, and I think his behaviour in the camp was motivated mostly by his determination that we be regarded as 'prisoners of war'. But, unfortunately, the Volunteers under him were miserable and dispirited. He would have driven them to desperation or into the British army. He instituted a procedure whereby Volunteers were punished by their own officers for what he regarded as breaches of discipline, by being confined to cells. However well-intentioned this was, it had a most depressing effect on Volunteers occupying that portion of the camp, especially on those of us who had recently endured solitary confinement at Knutsford. Fortunately, he was released early – he was of little danger except to us – and the rules he had drawn up were completely ignored. To the credit of the rest of our junior officers, they did not seek privileges; they ate the same rations, shared what they had and took responsibility with high purpose but an easy grace.

Eventually, those who remained in the camp were housed or billeted in the old distillery. There had been numerous releases, and our numbers were finally reduced to between 800 and 1,000. All courtesies to the British were omitted. It was the practice for the British commanding officer to address us at the morning parade and say, 'Good morning, men. Hats off.' But our main body were not long in the distillery before we refused to answer or pay him such courtesies. We just ignored him.

★ ★ ★

INSIDE THE GPO

A British-appointed commission to determine the cause of the Rising was sitting in Wormwood Scrubs Prison in London, and Volunteers were brought in batches from the camp to give evidence to the commission. Every possible encouragement was given to the Volunteers at that inquiry to declare that they had no previous knowledge of the Rising, and that they had been more or less 'misled'.

The commission was obviously trying to find evidence of 'German gold' or, alternatively, that the Volunteers had been led in ignorance into the Rising by their leaders. This is a curious historical fact. The British could not concede that all of us who had fought had lived our lives and worked towards that Easter Week in Dublin. Some of the Volunteers who were questioned at that inquiry were members of the Kimmage garrison and were liable for conscription, since they had normally resided in England. Five of these men were identified and then handed over to the military authorities in London. They did not return to Frongoch. Yet all the Kimmage garrison, including Mick Collins and myself, were liable for conscription, and the British authorities were well aware that a number of such wanted men were still in Frongoch.

It was decided amongst us by acclamation that no man would answer to his name if called by the authorities. What I believe was our first small cleavage began over that issue. During this whole period in Frongoch, the Citizen Army men sank their identity as a separate military body and had no special billets, officers or leaders. They accepted leadership from the Volunteers. But some Volunteers did not agree with the instruction not to answer names.

I was in a hut in the north camp when the doors were abruptly closed and, as suddenly, the soldiers of a kilted, Scottish regiment with fixed bayonets entered and confronted us. Their officer then started to read out names, and a few of our men did answer when called. But the majority of the men in that hut remained silent. Those of us who did not answer – about 300 in all, I think – were then marched to the lower camp, the distillery, where we all promptly went on hunger strike. After three or four days, we were allowed to rejoin our comrades in the rest of the camp, and eventually all the Volunteers were taken to the old distillery.

One of the results of our declining to answer names was unfortunate but inevitable. As a result of refusing to reveal our identities, we received no parcels and no messages from home. This was a great sacrifice, for nearly forty per cent of the prisoners were married men.

Meanwhile, the tribunal established by the British at Wormwood Scrubs was still sitting. They persisted in their expectation that more Volunteers would appeal against their internment, since they were still being held without trial, and many without any direct evidence that they had been involved in the Rising. Some of the non-belligerents had already been released, but the men from the Rising refused to take advantage of this. The British remained in a quandary. Batches of men who would not appeal were being taken to London.

I did not enjoy my own trip to Wandsworth Prison, under heavy guard, by train from Frongoch. Two of our London-Irish pals had been handed over to the military after appearing before that tribunal, and charged with desertion. They were two of our most determined men, the Nunan brothers, who had been sent over by their father from London to join in the Rising. The fight they were to put up saved the rest of the 'wanted men'. They each received fifty-six days on bread and water, and spent a lot of time in their underclothes, for when they were forced into British uniforms they promptly tore them off.

When my turn came to go to London, I was anxious not to be identified. When we arrived at Paddington Station, I got a huge shock when a girlfriend of mine from London suddenly called out my name. It was amazing and alarming that she recognised me. She called out two or three times. I ignored her.

I stuck to our agreed tactics, and did my damnedest to blacken myself before that tribunal. I had no desire to pit my strength against military discipline – having seen what happened to conscientious objectors. I was a very relieved man when I was taken back to Frongoch. The officer of the Welsh Guards in charge of us on the journey was a decent man. He provided us with newspapers, tactfully telling us first that Roger Casement had that day been hanged in Brixton Prison.

Back in Frongoch, however, we were not long left in peace. The authorities were still trying to locate the men liable to conscription. The rest of the prisoners would still not answer their names or numbers, and the next stage of the fight was on. It was a monotonous, dreary period. We were still confined to that derelict distillery, with men who could still not receive parcels or letters, since this would betray the identity of their comrades.

It was a grand passage in the history of Irish resistance to oppression. It is very hard to deny oneself letters under prison conditions. There was one case in particular that was especially noble. One of our older men, a member of the Citizen Army, very affectionately known as 'the Blackguard Daly', showed an amazing loyalty during our imprisonment. He was informed that his wife had died, leaving a number of young children. This ex-British army private soldier had served the greater part of his life in India. Though encouraged by Mick Collins to reveal his identity, and accept the privilege of returning to Dublin, he declined to do so. In case he might weaken us, he said he would not do it, and so he remained in the camp. The 'Blackguard Daly' was well known to the camp guards as a gentle man, and he did not know at that time how his children were circumstanced.

MICHAEL COLLINS IN FRONGOCH

A story had been started by some mean-spirited person
– by whom I cannot say – that the surrender in Moore
Street was brought about by members of the Kimmage garrison prevailing upon our GHQ to surrender. This couldn't
have been further from the truth, as the 'wanted men' of
the English-born contingent had, as I've already said, tried
desperately to persuade our leaders to fight to the finish.
I was hurt and indignant at this rumour. I felt that there
was no honourable alternative to my canvassing among the
'wanted men' to persuade them to surrender themselves. I
knew the rumour to be a vicious lie, for I'd spent those last
few hours with the staff before the surrender. (I did not
learn until much later, when an old comrade told me, that I
had aroused someone's jealousy with my very innocent cup
of tea for the staff.)

Absurd simple-minded gossip can stir up serious consequences. I let Mick Collins know that I'd asked my comrades
of the Kimmage garrison to surrender to the British, rather
than to adhere to a body of men who could believe such
gossip and deliberate lies.

Mick acted at once. That was my first experience of
Mick's judgement in leadership and love of the good name
of his country. But by now I was so pig-headed and touchy
that I'd decided to go and surrender myself, as also had

many of my comrades. Mick asked me not to do it. I said I would, and nothing could stop me.

He said, 'Joe, if you do this thing, you will shame us forever. I beg you not to do it.' But I remained determined. Then he said, sadly, 'It will be a blot on the name of Ireland for ever.'

I replied angrily that this lie was a blot on my own name, and on those of my closest friends. He then asked me to withhold any more action until he could call a full meeting of the whole camp. This he did instantly.

He assembled all Volunteers together in the dining hall, and addressed them. At that time, there were still Volunteers from every part of Ireland – including the Gaeltacht, the Irish-speaking parts of the country – and many did not yet know one another well. Mick said that the shameful lie about events in Moore Street might have been believed by some men, and might have weakened our solidarity if allowed to go unchecked. He spoke with passion of the particular sacrifice of the English-born Irishmen during the Rising, and put stress on our being chosen to fight in direct defence of the Commander-in-Chief. He was particularly emphatic when he came to their 'special courage and fierce reluctance to surrender at all!'

For the first time I was seeing a brilliant example of the genius for leadership in Michael Collins. He pointed out that we of the Kimmage garrison had had our share of

casualties, and that it was unthinkable that Irish-born Volunteers would agree to the surrender of such comrades to
the enemy.

At the end of his speech he was loudly cheered. And
that put a stop to an intrigue which, incidentally, was really
aimed at taking the natural leadership from those who had
it: that is, from Dick Mulcahy, Michael Collins and Gearoid
O'Sullivan. There had been as yet no attempt, so far as I can
remember, to appoint these men as our leaders. They led by
their natural gifts and that special ability they all had to instil
confidence in their followers.

Great-hearted Mick ... I had fought him always – and
always admired him. He knew men's and women's hearts and
how to move them. Of all the remarkable men I've had the
honour to call my comrades during this period, he was the
one with the stamp of greatness. My wife, May, was to meet
him on only one occasion. And her memory of that single
encounter – he asked her for a dance at a céilí – was treasured throughout her life. 'That Michael Collins,' she would
often say, 'once smiled at me.'

Once, in Frongoch, I watched Mick for a long time without his being aware of it. It was during the late dusk of
evening and long into the night. Mick was trying his best to
put a fifty-six-pound shot-weight over a high bar, a height
over which that same shot had been thrown very easily by
a strong Galwayman earlier that day. Mick tried and tried

– thinking himself alone – and at last he got it over. Then, seeing me there watching him, he said, 'And what do *you* think of that?'

'I'm just sorry,' I said to him. 'I wanted to see you break your back.' We both laughed and he gave me a bear hug.

From that period on, the Volunteers in Frongoch continued to be united in their determination to protect the Kimmage Company from the British. The camp worked smoothly. Our leaders all seemed to take their cue from Mick Collins. His aim was to give our captors all the annoyance possible. He took every opportunity to bribe our guards. The military guards were often replaced by men from another regiment or unit, but to no avail. Mick continued to corrupt them all. The British commandant addressed these newly recruited guards and told them that their predecessors had been 'corrupted' by the prisoners – meaning Mick – and then the new guards, or some of them, would make instant inquiries, asking, 'Who's the bloke what's 'anding out the bribes?'

We relieved the monotony by rough horseplay. Mick would stand on a staircase and tackle all coming or going to the dormitory above us. I don't know how he or I managed to survive it at times, for some of our opponents were very strong countrymen, who could have hurt us but for their good temper. Certainly, Mick and myself were not gentle. And his favourite remark to me, after some devilment, was,

'Joe – you'll be hanged yet.' Another man and myself often made some cups of supper cocoa and smuggled these in somehow to Mick and his group. Though they were the leaders of our dormitory, there was nothing formal or officious about them.

Once they were discussing economics and, as I was passing, I said to Mick, 'What the hell do *you* know about economics?' He almost jumped into the air. This was pretty chancey – I had read nothing then on the subject myself, and was a deal younger than Mick. I joked that some famous economist had spoken to me. I did not say it was a lecture Lenin had given in London. At least I knew that Lenin *could* be described as an economist, but that was all I knew on the topic at that time. To my surprise, Mick had also been to that same lecture. The Clonakilty lad had certainly got around.

Once, when an English officer came into our dining hall uttering threats, Mick routed him in a most un-Irish manner. He jumped immediately on to a table and shouted out things about that officer's personal character. To do violence to someone's sensibilities is not an Irish characteristic. Mick had learned that in England. He knew how to turn their own weapons against them. It is a saying in England that every man has his price – and Mick was to employ this weapon very effectively.

And yet – and I was always certain of this – the most significant characteristic about Mick Collins in his dealings with the English was that *he never disliked them*. If anything, he appreciated and enjoyed them. He was to defeat them in war, and to a large extent around the bargaining table later, *because* he understood them; he could match their manipulative tactics. He'd grown up working among them, from his time as a junior civil servant or as an insurance expert in London. Well-educated as he was, with a brilliant analytical mind, he was the first great modern Irishman who could match the British military and political leaders.

His supreme ease in bribing the Frongoch guards was one thing we often discussed. One evening, we sat in the sunshine watching a group of our guards near by. Mick looked at them a moment, and then jerked his head in that characteristic way and said, 'The nicest thing about the British soldier is his corruptibility.'

'Yes,' I agreed, 'he is the finest flower of English civilisation.'

'Ah, now that's *just* it,' said Mick. 'Every "Tommy" takes bribes like a gentleman.'

'You mean they're all traitors to their country?' I suggested.

'On the contrary,' Mick replied with a laugh, '"Tommy" has such complete confidence in the invincibility of that English "demi-paradise" that he has no compunction about hocking a little of its security to tide him over!'

Collins often demonstrated the truth of his judgement on the character of the guards. On one occasion, just before the dawn one morning, I overheard an entire conversation he'd had while bribing one of the English sergeants. I didn't have shorthand or I'd have got it down exactly; but I made notes afterwards and checked these over with Mick himself, who laughed heartily at my ingenuity and made some emendations to my 'copy', suggesting we keep it as 'a memento of "Our University Days"'![34]

It has been said that Frongoch was the greatest error the British could have made; that Frongoch became, effectively, a school of revolution. The main reason for this was that before the Rising, the 'hardcore' of the Volunteer movement had not worked – let alone fought – in close conjunction and comradeship. Frongoch welded us together, irrevocably. Also, there was a huge bonus in the recruitment to our movement of a large body of men that the British had, in their panic, incarcerated with that hardcore. Many of these new men, almost all born and bred in Ireland, had not participated in the Rising, or had only the remotest connection until now with the Volunteers. In Frongoch, they were infected with the virus of revolution. And so, the romantic dreams of a few young men from the Rising, many of

---

34 Many years later, while working on my play about Collins, *Hang the Bright Colours* (the Collins family had given me approval to cull that title from a letter by George Bernard Shaw to Michael's sister, Hannah), I wrote to my father, Joe, to ask his permission to dramatise an extension of this incident with Collins, which, though Joe had often described it to me, he'd never written down. When Joe later read these scenes, his comment was: 'By God, you could have been there too!'

whom had been born in exile, were to become the waking life of a whole people.

Men from all parts of Ireland had been sent to Frongoch. Sallow, tall, sombre men from Galway and the western seaboard; slow to converse, as if suspicious of men of the 'Pale', but true as steel and implacable against their traditional enemy. Men from the Golden Vale; gay and reckless. Men from Cork, city or county; hard-headed, fiery, touchy and aggressive, with a strong vein of realism. And Dubliners; good-natured, improvident and unambitious cosmopolitans.

I was to discover that provincial characteristics *did* really exist. I had thought it an expression of childish rivalry when I'd heard shouts of 'Up Cork!' or 'Up Kerry!' or 'Up Mayo!' But there was also that common Irish ingredient that made them indivisibly one – if attacked by the enemy, they would all stick together. There were a few with ambition but lacking ability; and a few little men lacking compassion, bitter and spiteful, with a knowledge of Gaelic but impervious to culture, who had been soured by the gall and wormwood of foreign oppression, but who were not lacking in courage. And then there were those others who felt slighted that they had *not* been sentenced to death, feeling that they deserved the martyr's crown.

In another age or country, these men would have sought glory. Some did. A few others, most dangerous of all, were like children to whom religion and nationality were synonymous.

These asked only for orders, and they would do the most menial jobs. To these, an oath would be sacred, never to be forsworn. One such man[35] was to die facing an Irish firing squad twenty-four years later, British bullets still in his body, condemned to death by a court martial authorised by a government headed by Eamon de Valera.

Occasionally, Volunteers were taken under guard to the local town for dental treatment, and full advantage was taken of these occasions to make sure that carefully prepared propaganda was smuggled out of the camp. Much was made of our 'confined' sleeping space – the area in cubic feet allotted to each man was minimised – although in fact, on the whole, the Volunteers' health was good.

Indeed, a military doctor said that our camp was unique in his experience, for amongst 1,800 men he did not find a single case of venereal disease. One of our more facetious comrades said, on hearing this, that we were in danger of not being considered a real army under such circumstances, and that he would personally take measures to see that our situation or reputation was redeemed – but I have no evidence that he succeeded.

It's a sad fact that the continued publicity about our long alleged insanitary quarters caused the camp doctor, who was a civilian, to commit suicide; a victim of circumstances, he was torn between military orders, our propaganda and professional

---

35 Joe would never tell me this man's name.

etiquette. The commandant paraded us and upbraided us for this man's death. Being a high churchman himself, he mentioned the word catholic and nearly precipitated a riot, because the Volunteers broke ranks and, notwithstanding the guards, approached him and swore at him, and then turned their backs on him, never to parade again. From that day forward, he never addressed us, and we disobeyed every order. The instigator of this annoyance, of course, was Mick Collins, always in his element making war on something or someone. But though he was conspicuous in all the tussles with our warders, he was never disliked by them.

During our stay in Frongoch we were not especially conscious of our leaders, because Dick Mulcahy, Gearoid O'Sullivan and Michael Collins did not form a clique, but played and worked with all. The men in Frongoch were a band of brothers. I was dependent on the loyalty and self-sacrifice of these men not to betray my English origin, and I was never, but once, made conscious of it.

The six or eight Kimmage garrison men who had been taken from us were handed over to the British army. All of them, including the two Nunan brothers, three King brothers and Paddy O'Donoghue, were eventually to be discharged from the British army, as 'persons not likely to give loyal and faithful service to His Majesty' – a delicious understatement about men who had taken up arms *against* His Majesty for a week in Dublin city.

INSIDE THE GPO

When the main body of our men in the camp were denied access to playing fields, many turned to carving bones and making rings out of coins. Some larger meat-bones became astonishing sculptures. In one instance, an immense bone became a Celtic cross. Poets we were not. The only poems by revolutionaries worthy of the name in that period were by the poets among our leaders whom the enemy had shot after the Rising. But though our verse was puny, some products were not, as we had quite a clutch of artists and craftsmen amongst us.

The more boisterous played indoors, especially the game that I christened 'Dead Man'. I can claim to have contrib-uted something to 'the National Effort', having invented that game.

One man stood in a circle of others, stiff as a mummy, and allowed himself to be pushed across the circle from one side to the other; he who failed to catch and return the body became 'Dead Man'. This adventure provided indoor exer-cise and amusement, and needed a certain amount of nerve.

Some of the most obstreperous of us were positive pests, but we were tolerated by the dormitory leaders, serious elderly men who took our high spirits in good part. Once I thought I had gone too far by accidentally flooding Dick Mulcahy's dormitory. The guard was turned out and marched into Dick's apartment. Dick was asked, 'What was the cause of this disorder?' Dick replied, 'Too much water!'

A modest appraisal, as the place was awash. But I was not admonished, nor did Dick say a word to me, though he knew I was the culprit. O wise young men – who knew it was better by far to have pests than dangerous apathy.

But it was still a wretched time, for all of our apparent high spirits. I was ever conscious of the threat that hung over me, that I would be picked out and have to go through the ordeal of defying the British army alone; and wondering if my courage would sustain me when my time came. One weak man would destroy all. Yet those pinpricks of military despotism were answered by our national genius for provocation. How those military must have hated us. Try as they would, they were worsted. And it would all have been so easy and simple if they had left us our rags of uniforms and called us prisoners of war, but they regarded us as a mob and, by God, they got a mob.

All the prisoners were informed that they would be released on 22 or 23 December 1916. All was ready and the train was waiting, but then we were all asked to give our names, so that tickets could be issued to us for our journey. We all refused to give our names or addresses. For a terrible moment, it must have seemed to our captors that they would never be able to get rid of us. The tickets, after much debate, were handed over en bloc, and were distributed among the men.

So we were released for Christmas of 1916. The British stated that they regarded this as a gesture of reconciliation, but the Volunteers had no such illusions. We knew that we had bit the hand that fed us so badly it was glad to release us. The men all believed, and they were proven right in this, that they had irrevocably intimidated Whitehall and Downing Street.

HOME FOR CHRISTMAS

PADDY MCGRATH TOOK me with him to Dublin. Ireland was now home to me, as Dublin was to be my city. Hospitality, given or received, is a sacred thing. For the next five years, I must have been sheltered in dozens of homes in Dublin and the south of Ireland.

So far I had been but three months in Ireland, up to the end of the Rising, and would never (except on active duty) leave it again. Yet it was to be that first few years, in my own country at last, which became for me the most dear and indelible time of my whole life. And I would not consciously lie or exaggerate whilst remembering any part of it.

The internees from Frongoch arrived from England at the North Wall, on the River Liffey in Dublin. There were few people to meet us, because the authorities had concealed the time and place of our arrival. I doubt in any case whether many Dubliners would have met us at that stage; but from the time of our return, a change was taking place in the city. O'Connell Street (still called Sackville Street, still in ruins and looking sacked) was then a place where one could walk with freedom, and it was being paraded by numbers of young men. At that time there was so little motor traffic that there was a great deal of room for casual strollers in the streets. The ruins we had left behind to mark our passage there were still very evident, but so were the earliest stages of reconstruction and rebuilding; no doubt the authorities were well aware of the dangers of leaving such evidence for conjecture and appraisal.

There was a comic context to much of this. Normally, Dubliners would have just rambled about, but now they appeared to march. They had acquired the new habit of keeping step, and on greeting each other gave an indifferent military salute. It was a curiously ironic fact that these citizens sometimes unknowingly saluted the very men who had fought in these ruins that lay about us.

We were in rags, but the 'Prisoners' National Fund'[36] soon provided us with ready-made suits. And I got a job at once on the *Freeman's Journal* – the newspaper that had been burned down in Abbey Street, behind the GPO, in Easter Week. That job lasted only a fortnight. I was not yet a qualified electrician, and could not have lived on

---

. 36 Irish National Aid Fund.

apprentice wages – even if anyone would have me.

Mick Collins was secretary of the National Fund. I had already informed him that I was working, but I now had to approach him again, having nothing to live on. The previous day I had been given a lunch in a hotel by one of the more prosperous Volunteers.

Mick asked me what I wanted. I said, 'You know damn well.'

He said, 'But I saw you taking lunch at the Red Bank yesterday.'

I said, 'And who paid for *your* bloody lunch?' and I marched out of the room.

But he sent me one pound per week, the usual sum paid to victimised Volunteers. I refused to sign for or accept it, but eventually was glad to take it, although without signing. This must have been one of the few occasions when Mick did *not* demand – or receive – a receipt.

There was a sequel to this. Near Christmas 1917, an open cheque for twenty-five pounds was sent to me, made payable to Joe A. O'Doog, and the banks could not open quick enough for me to cash it. Months later, Mick asked me, 'Did you get a cheque?'

'No,' said I, 'but someone with a name close enough to mine managed to cash it.'

Mick laughed at me: he knew his man. He told me it was my share from when he'd wound up the National Prisoners' Funds.

That fund was necessary and performed an important task, because a large number of Volunteers were victimised by their employers. One outstanding case was that of the National University, from which Harry Walpole was discharged by the then president of the university. As far as I know, no student attending that university seemed to be aware of the dismissal or commented on the matter.

REORGANISATION OF THE VOLUNTEERS, 1917

Early in 1917, the Dublin Brigade of the Irish Volunteers was reorganised. I became a member of the C Company 2nd Battalion, which was to be immediately under the command of our GHQ. Dick McKee[37] was officer commanding the battalion; one of the two brothers Meldon was captain of C Company, the other brother being lieutenant. Our headquarters were in Gloucester Street.

The first orders we received were rather ambiguous. We were told to 'raid for arms', but also ordered 'not to fire on the police' – the RIC. On one occasion, myself and Tommy Kearns, having successfully raided a house for arms, had to hide around corners from policemen, with arms in our hands. A good deal of raiding was carried out during this early period and, as far as I know, no shooting incidents resulted. Meanwhile young Dublin lads (not in the

---

37 McKee was commandant of the Dublin Brigade, 1918–20.

Volunteers) continued to march the streets with that military stride and flutters of salute. It was sheer comedy. A large number of Volunteers had acquired revolvers, which they sometimes carried about on everyday business, though few of these men had any intention of using them.

The Irish Volunteers had earned an extraordinary reputation for piety and sobriety. As a result, numbers of 'Sinn Féin'[38] clubs sprang up, Sinn Féin being the compendious term first used by the Irish, and later by the enemy, to designate the many patriotic bodies throughout the country. These clubs were all anxious to purchase huge patriotic banners and impedimenta, and this cottage industry provided a living for a few Volunteers-turned-artists.

By March 1917, quite a number of us had acquired guns, with still, for the most part, no intention of using them – though they made one feel fine. We began secret drilling in working men's clubs, referring to the company drill hall as 'The Club'. Every funeral, including those where the deceased had only the most tenuous relationship to the movement, and at times none at all, became an excuse for a parade. Dublin had become the City of Parades. Meanwhile, private residences continued to be raided for arms, with little result except an occasional shotgun. Raids continued to be carried out with courtesy and without violence.

But things were beginning to hot up. On one occasion,

---

38 Sinn Féin: 'Ourselves' in Irish.

a Volunteer with wet feet, having avoided policemen by hiding the arms he had acquired on a raid in a doorway, got fed up waiting and stopped a smart car driven by a chauffeur, and said, 'Home, James.' James did as he was told without argument ...[39] This state of affairs could not go on forever – even for the most illogical of people. We were in danger of losing any little enthusiasm we possessed. In fact, the revolutionary movement was all but dead, but for the IRB in the background, out of sight and knowledge of most of us.

But the *spirit* of what had made the insurrection of 1916 had spread throughout the country, an intangible mood, composed of gallantry, gaiety and irony, rarely grim: the songs and ballads and stories were teasing or ironical and ended with laughter. The ranting, pompous patriotic poem was an anachronism and indulged in and borne only with deep embarrassment. A twentieth-century political renaissance, it was analogous with the Irish literary renaissance that had helped it into being. But, if you asked, later, any of those concerned what they best remembered of that time, it would be something humorous, even when things had become – as they did soon enough – deadly grim. The best jokes were those we told against ourselves. This one is typical: It happened soon after our surrender in Easter Week. There was

---

39 I always suspected and often asked my father if it were he who had become impatient on that wet night. He'd just smile and say nothing, so I knew it was Joe who, just for once, took the easy road home.

one member of James Connolly's staff, a very small youth; utterly honest, he had carried the 'war-purse' – some thousands of pounds in cash to pay for 'requisitions' – and he had kept this very large sum in his humble home. The idea of putting the money in banks did not occur to him; if it had, he would not have trusted them. He had a lot of gold braid on his beautiful uniform, and he was accoutred with a fine sword. He was the picture of a very little chocolate soldier. James Connolly tolerated him, with that special gentleness he possessed for children and women.

This much-emblazoned small adjutant, gold braid and all, escaped up a chimney when his post was taken by the British in the final assault. From his hiding place, he heard the attackers lamenting the men they had lost in the battle, so he delayed his appearance amongst them until he was exhausted and almost unconscious. A kind Tommy gave him a drink of whiskey – the first drop in his abstemious life – and it all but killed him. In this condition, half choking on whiskey, with his scabbard dangling, he was carried to a room in which a number of condemned Volunteer leaders were held. The British sergeant who carried him dropped him on the floor with a clatter, saying, 'Here's your ... brigadier general!'

One of our leaders who was condemned to death – it was John MacBride – when asked by a comrade some distance away what the sentence of the military court was, made the sign of a circle with his pipe over his heart and replaced it in his mouth. He'd fought the British anywhere he could for years, including South Africa during the Boer War.

Before they shot him, they tried to bandage his eyes. MacBride said, 'Why bother? I have been looking down your rifle-barrels all my life.' And a little later, a young boy – I think it was Pearse's younger brother, Willie – would toss and catch his hat on his way to that same execution wall.

There were a couple of other stories of Easter Week that I've always enjoyed; in fact, relished so much that I've never shared them until now. It was Colonel Joe Byrne who told me this one: He had returned from South Africa himself just before the Rising, but although he wasn't a Volunteer and hadn't been mobilised, he was a member of the IRB. Easter Monday caught him by surprise, and on hearing the guns, he proceeded to put his affairs in order. On the following day, Tuesday, he reported to the GPO. On entering, he saw his old friend, Joe Stanley, later owner of the Drogheda Argus and other provincial newspapers, who said to him, 'Hadn't you the bloody sense to know you should keep out of this?'

Byrne's reply was, 'No more sense than yourself by the looks of this.'

Neither Stanley nor Byrne was serving in the Volunteers; neither was subject to any mobilisation; but both were active

IRB men, and were what would now be referred to as fifth-columnists,[40] since both occupied respectable positions in society but were subversives belonging to a secret society.

My favourite story involved Captain Frank Mullen, who was in charge of a section that occupied Boland's Mill on Easter Monday. He halted his company on the bridge, told the men they were about to go into action, and concluded, 'Any Volunteer who wishes may hand over his rifle and leave our ranks.' Whereupon, one Volunteer at once dropped his rifle and bolted.

A Volunteer sergeant standing beside Captain Mullen sighted his rifle on the fleeing man and said, 'Shall I drop him, Sir?' – upon hearing which, another Volunteer standing in the ranks spun on his heel and fainted flat on the road.

Much later still, at the height of the actions against the British secret service, when Mick Collins had ordered the sweep in which they were wiped out, there was a bizarre incident. One member of our Active Service Unit in Dublin entered the bedroom of a British intelligence officer, and said to him gently, whilst sitting on his bed, 'Where's your gun, Mac?' 'Mac' shortly thereafter had no further use for guns.

All these men, young and old, especially the members of our Active Service Unit, appeared to have carried their adolescence into manhood, had become 'lords of beauty and of

---

40 Members of an organised group within a country at war, working for the enemy; originally, in the Spanish Civil War.

loving laughter' in preparing to die for their country. It was an unbelievable time. People who had money lent big sums without a receipt. All borrowed each other's property as if it was communal. The only thing a Volunteer would steal was arms, and our politicians stole only each other's thunder. It's worth looking up the manifesto of the first elected Sinn Féin gathering: an only equivalent expression of revolutionary solidarity can be found in the Communist Manifesto, which might to some extent have influenced the Sinn Féin manifesto.

SINN FÉIN

MY FIRST EXPERIENCE of politicians, and the new Irish politics that led to the formation of the Sinn Féin (Ourselves Alone) party, was soon to follow. I can't remember the exact date of the meeting held in the Mansion House with that purpose. It was probably early April of 1917.[41] We held this gathering to formulate a party and a policy, just a year from the date of the Rising. Count Plunkett, Gavan Duffy and Arthur Griffith were on the platform, a trio that I thought was guaranteed to cause a conflagration. I went with high expectations and a little trepidation, expecting a rough night. It certainly was rough.

Plunkett was chairman, tall and dignified with white beard and clear complexion. No sash was needed to proclaim him a Knight of the Holy Roman Empire. The Count, whose three sons had embraced martyrdom, was impatient of

---

41 19 April 1917.

temperate men or means. He tried and failed to suppress his indignation with the pacifist, Arthur Griffith, who was sitting close beside him. One of Plunkett's sons, Joseph, had been executed and two more of his sons were still in prison.

Griffith sat there like a sphinx, square and solid, like a man of granite, lacking charm – physically or mentally. Griffith had a mind of ice that could freeze Irish histrionic champagne solid. He was the one cold fact in a sea of fantasy, a fact that could not be liked or ignored. The Volunteers disliked him and scorned him. Any other revolutionaries would have pushed him aside ruthlessly: and in their unwillingness to push him aside lay the weakness and the strength of the Volunteers. They were too chivalrous to attack Griffith in his isolation, yet believed him to be a menace who should be dealt with. There would be other Volunteers like Collins who knew how to deal with facts, and they would prove, ironically, to be Griffith's best defenders.

The meeting was not long in progress before the two extremes clashed: Plunkett, the romanticist, angry and accusing; Griffith cold, rational, obdurate. Gavan Duffy, moderate, exquisitely dressed, but outclassed, was in the middle trying to play the mediator, but such was Count Plunkett's mounting anger that serious disturbance was inevitable. I think everyone at the meeting fully expected that the men on the platform would remain irreconcilable, and Duffy's attempts to intervene were in vain – it was a fight between two giants.

Strangers were on their feet, taking notes in the audience. I thought they were detectives. There were many Volunteers in the hall, and thinking we were dealing with G-men[42], we snatched their books and pencils – and then realised that the note-takers were journalists.

By standing up to take notes they had, fortunately, killed the most exciting story of the day. This commotion in the audience caused a useful diversion; those on the platform had time to think, and they invited the journalists on to the platform. But for that very lucky incident, Plunkett would have precipitated a riot. My personal sympathies were with the Count. I remembered Joe Plunkett on that lonely street during the Rising. And gentle, brave George Plunkett, who had walked out into that hail of machine-gun bullets in Moore Street to pick up a wounded Tommy. The two forces, rationalism and romanticism, had met for the first time. It would not be the last encounter between the opposing forces of the revolution.

THE LONGFORD ELECTION

There were, I believe, two elections during 1917. Count Plunkett won the first seat.[43] Our tactic was simple. If the new Sinn Féin party could take the seats, those elected

---

42 Detectives from G-Division of British Intelligence, Dublin Castle.

43 North Roscommon by-election, February 1917.

would refuse to go to Westminster, and would take their place at home in the new national assembly of Dáil Éireann. Our candidate in County Longford was Joe McGuinness, who was still in prison, and he'd be contesting a seat in an entrenched and virulent unionist area. Any available Volunteers were urged to help him in this tough campaign.

Four of us cycled to Longford. How we were going to live, we never asked; but with borrowed bikes and a shilling or so in our pockets, we took to the road, and arrived in the town of Longford dead beat next day, having lost ourselves in Leitrim on the way. We did our best to get Joe McGuinness elected as MP, and had a hectic couple of days. The ladies McGuinness looked after us, seeing that we had beds and food. Everyone worked round the clock, and when the poll was counted, we were beaten by a few votes. We were tired out. The unionist parliamentary party went mad with their victory. There was one man amongst us who was *not* so dead beat, however. Joe McGrath, who some years later founded the Irish Sweepstakes, then demonstrated his genius for mathematics. Joe demanded and got a recount, and to our amazement, McGuinness was declared elected for Sinn Féin, by a majority of thirty-seven or thereabouts.[44]

It was not a clean sweep, yet, but that was *two seats* taken from the reactionary party. There was another worthwhile bonus on that trip; the first sign that the RIC might be

---

44 He won by thirty-nine votes, after two recounts.

affected by the national resurgence was when I saw police-men joking, drinking and 'colloguing' with our Volunteers.

On our long cycle back to Dublin it was roses, roses, all the way. We had tricolour flags of green, white and orange on our handlebars, a rare sight then in Ireland, for it was the flag of the insurrection. I cycled behind a lad with long, golden, curly hair, which was lifted by the breeze; the sun was reflected in his face as he sang. We all sang of freedom with him.

Nineteen-seventeen was a year of marching: mostly we marched to funerals. The funeral of Thomas Ashe was to be the climax of these. It was a tremendous affair, in which thou-sands marched who had never marched before or marched since. But more of that event later.

Infantrymen loathe marching, but how young Dublin men seemed to love it. On the least excuse, a column of fours would appear – not Volunteers, or just a few among them perhaps, but young Dublin men, intoxicated by the rhythmic sound of marching feet; they fell into lines and followed. I thought that if it had been possible to lead them to a drill hall, they would have taken a soldier's oath, and if equipped, might have been as good troops as any.

The first serious event in the obstruction of British administration on the part of my battalion was a seizure of pigs, which would otherwise have been taken to the North Wall for export. This amusing job was handled excellently by the out-of-work men of my section, Volunteers who were nicely qualified for the work. It was decided to seize this drove of pigs as a protest against the unrestricted export of livestock. We seized our prey, and drove them to the Corporation abattoir. They were killed and dressed by some experts amongst us. It is a terribly messy business, killing pigs. The police collected in force outside the slaughterhouse, and Volunteers occasionally appeared at the doors of the abattoir – very bloody, with long knives in their hands.

It reminded me of Thomas Carlyle's image of the Septembrists in his *History of the French Revolution*. The police were, however, not at all anxious to assert their authority. The owner of the pigs was compensated, I believe, and a bacon-curer was found to accept the slaughtered pigs. We escorted them through the city streets to this purchaser. That was one procession I enjoyed.

Bizarre events abounded throughout the city. An army tank – like those used against us in Easter Week – was patrolling near Mountjoy Prison. It was intended to intimidate the people, no doubt, which was very foolish, for they were the usual curious crowd which will collect anywhere on a Sunday. The tank moved up and down the road like some son of blind mastodon, and then halted, with a Tommy looking out of the turret. A citizen with two young children stood to look at the tank: Father taking the children for a Sunday walk whilst Mother prepared the dinner. Father had his Sunday-best clothes on and, that sign of the very respectable Dubliner, he was carrying a walking stick. He stepped out in front of the tank, and deliberately, and without any hurry, broke the two headlamps with his stick, and then stepped back on the pavement to examine his handiwork. I saw the British Tommy struggling to find something to say, and I grinned – as did that citizen no doubt, when he told the story later. A more active form of coercion was necessary to deal with such a people.

★ ★ ★

But Thomas Ashe was dead, or dying, as a result of forced feeding in prison. Immediately before he died, he was taken to the Mater Hospital. Michael Collins, as organiser of our intelligence, and his fiery comrade Cathal Brugha worked in efficient unity on the massive funeral arrangements. Closest of friends, they were to be divided on the issue of the Treaty, and to be pitted against each other tragically in the Civil War. They could both be rash men, and on this occasion they did what I considered a rather reckless thing.

A huge mob of people were milling outside Mountjoy Gaol; they had worked themselves up almost into a state of hysteria by praying, singing and demonstrating. Mick and Cathal at that critical moment arrived on a horse-drawn side-car to address the crowd – and precipitated something of a riot.

Cathal Brugha was speaking from the side-car. Armed policemen stood in front of the prison gate, to prevent Cathal or his audience from approaching too near to it. There was a large column of young men marching in the vicinity, including – I noticed – that little group of young Volunteers who had discussed the hereafter in Moore Street in Easter Week, that small clutch of self-styled cynics. It looked, now, as if they could encounter the hereafter at any instant.

These young survivors of the Rising put themselves at the head of the column of marching men, realising that they could overwhelm and disarm the police if the column followed, as they were twenty to one against the police, whose revolvers were awkwardly positioned for quick withdrawal. Word was passed down the column to prepare to charge. Some men fell out of the press, but the pace was increased to a quick step, and suddenly the column turned the corner to confront the police and charge. The main body of the column halted, broke and melted away, but the first two files that ran at the police were buffeted and kicked out into the crowd, and Cathal's side-car was nearly turned over in the melee. Those young die-hards were now sorer, wiser men. Yet a couple of weeks later, one of those same young Volunteers, acting on impulse when Brugha was about to be arrested, swung his hurley-stick and killed a police inspector stone dead. It was strange how violence always followed Cathal.

FUNERAL OF THOMAS ASHE

Thomas Ashe's body, escorted by Volunteers, was taken to be lain in state in the City Hall – the City Hall that was itself next door to Dublin Castle, the seat of the British administration in Ireland. Indeed, the British military were themselves garrisoned not only in the Castle but also in the City Hall.

This led to one of the most audacious actions of the period. Notwithstanding the proximity of British troops, Thomas Ashe's remains were to be escorted from the City Hall by armed Volunteers in uniform. This piece of impudence would have brought the British into action against us but, I believe, for the ability of Richard Mulcahy, who carefully organised every detail of that eventful state funeral. The danger ended only when he carefully demobilised our Dublin Brigade within the walls of Glasnevin Cemetery. The whole operation was brilliantly executed.

In the centre of City Hall, Thomas Ashe lay dead, dressed in an officer's uniform of the Volunteers, surrounded by his guard of honour, also in uniform. Encircling the guard was a ring of marble statues, still stained with the blood of Volunteers, blood that had fallen from the roof barely eighteen months before. It was a round-the-clock guard, and that night vigil among blood-stained statues must have been a weird experience.

Richard Mulcahy was in a large room off City Hall, in charge of the funeral parade. He was writing at a table when a Volunteer officer fidgeting in front of him said, 'You wanted me, Sir ... What do you require, Sir?'

Mulcahy said, 'Please get out of my light.'

There was considerable tension. Our firing-party of Volunteers entered the huge hall to escort the body to the hearse and then to Glasnevin Cemetery. As the catafalque was being brought from the building, British officers were looking out of the windows.

The march began. I thought it a very risky thing to march with rifles in a procession consisting mainly of civilians. A big section of the Dublin Fire Brigade were participants; I smiled to think that their function was to damp down fires. It was an enormous cortège, representative of all parts of the country, led by a Volunteer contingent that was apt to be nervous.

Catastrophe almost occurred. One man who, I knew, was never a serving Volunteer (he never obeyed or gave orders) was in the parade in front of a number of men. He was dressed in an officer's uniform, although I knew he had not taken part in the Rising. A British military lorry driver, becoming impatient at the long funeral procession, attempted to drive through the cortège. The false 'officer' panicked, and a proportion of the procession was breaking up in disorder, fearing that the military were about to fire on or confront us.

Fortunately a very real Volunteer officer (later a close friend of mine), Joe Leonard, drew his revolver, ordered the military back, and restored calm in the procession. That false 'officer' was lucky to be in a situation where he could not be adequately dealt with; Joe Leonard completely spiked his guns later. The man in question was a literary gent and quite miscast in a military role in any circumstances. But Leonard made subsequent history; I saw this incident from a distance and realised that the 'hardcore' of Volunteers, which was to become the 'Squad'[45] – of whom Joe Leonard was to be one – had already formed.

THE VOLUNTEERS – SPIRIT AND MORALE

During that year of 1917, large numbers of Volunteers were without employment because of victimisation. There was irony in the fact that unemployed men were given the most risky tasks, which might entail imprisonment – and often did.

During the various election campaigns of 1917 and 1918, I was impressed by several things relating to the Volunteers. A very large number of men had come from the south of Ireland. Many were under the command of the Brennans.

---

45 The 'Squad', sometimes known as the 'Twelve Apostles', was a rotating group of men specially operating for Michael Collins, who mainly used them to execute British agents, informers, etc.

Paddy Brennan was the senior officer in the southern counties at that time. It was significant that the counties nearer to Dublin were not as well represented. A large number of Volunteers were from Dublin, but they were mostly unemployed.

The Volunteers from the south were dangerously enthusiastic. They were spoiling for a fight, and apt to be reckless. Whenever mobilised, they lent muscular as well as moral support during elections. On a return journey to Clare after some election work, as one company passed through Amiens Street Station on their way back from the north, they fired a number of shots through the glass roof, and probably through the roofs of other stations en route to their home towns. During these elections, fares were paid by our GHQ and the Volunteers were more than adequately catered for. It was the only occasion that the finance department of the movement (i.e. Mick Collins) did not appear to be niggardly.

The Dublin Volunteers were, for the most part, men who had been in action and associated with each other for a couple of years at least. The Dublin Brigade Volunteers were trained, experienced and disciplined, and possessed the prestige and satisfaction that a successful military action confers, if we regard the 1916 Rising as a success. But the Dublin Brigade had not recruited much new blood. A man's character is not as well known in a city as it would be in the country. Southerners felt that they had been let down in 1916 by the demobilisation order made by Eoin MacNeill, and they were impatient to justify themselves. I had heard in jail, and again in Longford and Armagh, something of the bitterness that was felt in the south about their inaction during the Rising.

After one election, I was very relieved to part with my responsibility – which had been the command of a section of the County Clare Volunteers. I assumed that the general enthusiasm of newly recruited Volunteers in Clare was the rule over the greater part of Ireland. Young men were wrought up to a pitch of enthusiasm to attack the enemy, but lacked everything except courage. The Volunteers had just enough arms to precipitate their own slaughter. There was no thought at that time of waging guerrilla warfare. This came later, with the Active Service Unit under the leadership of Collins and Brugha. Meanwhile, it was still a period of marching, on any occasion, in Dublin.

There was a tendency then for Volunteers to wear trench-coats. They were serviceable during our manoeuvres. In my one interview with de Valera, I suggested that what the Volunteers required was some sort of uniform. De Valera told me that he had designed a trench-coat that would have pockets in which the necessaries to take the field could be carried. But I was wrong, and so was he, in this: the days of marching in fours were over. We wanted arms first, last and all the time. Only Mick Collins saw this clearly. And I had had clear proof of Collins' foresight. As far back as early 1917, just after our release from Frongoch, I was speaking to Mick when we were interrupted by an American visitor who flourished a cheque-book and was offering Collins a cheque, or cash if he preferred. But Mick replied, angrily and rudely, 'We don't need your bloody money, we want guns! And more guns!' I said later that surely the money could have been used to buy guns, but Mick insisted that supply of arms (and not the means to pay for them) was our great problem.

During early 1918, I attended my company parades. A ludicrous attempt was made to drill with broomsticks, which I thought ridiculous. But often we did not even attempt this elementary foot-drill in our company halls, when the police were thought to be active. On occasions when the Volunteers carried out any new activities, or the British authorities seemed more threatening, our numbers on parade increased. Action – or just the chance of some – always strengthened resolve and raised the militants' hopes. This was so during the time when the Conscription Act was being debated in England, when all companies paraded in their fullest strength.

There was a feeling of tension during the conscription crisis at our meetings, but I cannot remember hearing of any plan as to how the Volunteers, as a military body, proposed fighting against conscription if and when it became operative in Ireland.

At that stage the Volunteers could not have fought very

effectively. They would have been slaughtered. The lack of arms was no one's fault. The few arms we had possessed had been taken from us after the Rising in 1916, and they were never so plentiful again until the British departed in 1922. In my opinion, it is impossible to train men as soldiers without arms, and that accounted for the decline in the number of men on parade, and of Volunteers everywhere in Ireland. As things stood, the Volunteers were a danger only to themselves.

TEA-TIME WITH DE VALERA

Before moving on to the most crucial event of 1918, however, perhaps it's worth going back to tell of that one encounter I had with Dev, and how much he amazed me later.

Though I've never voted for his party since it took power in the thirties, and though he was so fundamental a cause of the split over the Treaty – as the implacable foe of Mick Collins – and brought us all to the horror of Civil War, I have always admired and respected Eamon de Valera.

De Valera's huge popularity and personal myth sprang from the indisputable evidence of his courage during the Rising. He was among the last, if not the last, of the commanders to lay down arms. There is the probably apocryphal story of how he received the instruction to cease fire from Pearse and Connolly with the words, 'Ah, well ... Now I suppose I'll have to go back to school-teaching!' His air of academic distinction had always moved me. We all knew that he'd managed to inflict the only significant casualties on the British army during Easter Week.

From his command of the strategically important outposts at Mount Street Bridge and Boland's Mill, he had halted all advance of British reinforcements on their way into the city from the Dun Laoghaire direction. Knowing he had few, if any, good shots among his men, he insisted that they hold their first volleys until they could see not merely the whites of their enemies' eyes, but their pupils, and buttonholes.

In fact, I've long thought that it was the severity of British losses in that battle that persuaded their top brass to unleash artillery, firing both high explosive and incendiary shells. Such a determined and skillful opponent probably convinced them, erroneously, that this was a typical taste of what they would encounter on getting closer to our GHQ. Which may have been why our leaders chose such a zealot for this obvious hot-seat in the early strategy: perhaps Joe Plunkett's – or was it MacDonagh's planning? I had heard some stories of how Dev's men, nervous fingers itching and strained on those doubtful triggers, waited, and waited – it seemed forever – before hearing at last that quiet, restrained, calculated order: 'Now ... boys ... Fire ...'

I was sent to Dev with a dispatch, soon after his release from Lewes Prison. He had been among those condemned to be shot, but his Spanish-American father and US passport had reprieved him.

Dev was taking tea in a modest hotel, alone, although the room was crowded with well-wishers and supporters. This immensely tall (even sitting down he seemed to be standing), very lean, scholarly gentleman with, even then, extremely thick-lensed glasses, asked me to join him and take tea. At that time I was still an ordinary Volunteer, and felt a bit foolish. A 'reception committee of one', I thought at that moment. It was something like a private audience with the Pope; but then, this man could and often does still inspire a kind of reverence. Dev was very simple and courteous, but (or so it seemed to me at the time) lacked a capacity of putting men at their ease.

Dev urgently needed knowledge of the Volunteers, and I told him that the battalions were reforming and drilling. He then asked me what was the most pressing requirement. I said, some sort of uniform that could be easily donned or doffed, suggesting a trench-coat in which pockets and a haversack were incorporated, with a pocket for field-dressing. It was then, with a very slight smile, and perhaps a touch of pedantry, that he informed me that he had 'already designed just such a garment – when I was in prison'. We discussed, I remember clearly, our belief that the failure of other risings, including the Wexford rebellion, could be attributed – at least in some measure – to the lack of a military uniform.

But, on later reflection about our exchange of ideas on this question, I became convinced that we were still both under the influence of romantics. Not six months after that talk with Dev, I realised that a 'hardcore' of realists was necessary. I saw more and more signs from then on of the men who became that 'hardcore'.

My own romantic illusions up to then, as a Volunteer, had been of little consequence or danger to anyone. But Dev's illusion – or more aptly, delusion – as a major figure of that period, that an open, full-scale battle and an old-fashioned military campaign were possible, drove us to disaster and schism after the British withdrawal from the Twenty-six Counties.

But, on that afternoon, he was unassuming, kindly, courteous, and that was all I could make out from meeting and speaking to him. I was unimpressed by the audience, but a few days later he gave me a very big shock.

I can vividly remember de Valera's first major public speech in O'Connell Street. O'Connell Street was as packed that day as it had been before only for Jim Larkin. Dev told us he had been sent into the country before the originally intended nationwide Rising planned for Easter Week. His orders were to demobilise the country Volunteers units 'on an order from our GHQ', but on his return he found the insurrection decided upon, and thought that decision was wrong, to fight with such reduced forces. 'But of course I obeyed orders,' said Dev, to take the men under his command into action on Easter Monday. Dev went on to stress that he now saw that the leaders of the insurrection were right, and added: 'For the future I will demand a full Republic!' This, of course, is not a verbatim report but the main gist of what he said.

But it was that outspoken reference to 'the Republic' that gave me an increased respect for him – mixed with not a little awe. I was shocked and frightened. Our fat was at last in the fire. For how was a Republic to be achieved, except by a prolonged and a relentless struggle? And our Volunteers, God help them, having just luckily escaped ridicule and annihilation, must now face the consequences of this irrevocable spoken word. I knew that the cheering crowd did not realise what would be called for, but for those of us who did, and believed in the idea of a Republic, it spelled the danger of many deaths.

For the first time since the Proclamation of the Irish Republic by Pearse, outside the Post Office on Easter Monday morning, a major figure had stated publicly that he would not be satisfied with anything less than that Republic. To my mind the importance of what he said was that it welded together all the political parties, who put different tags on themselves, into a single party with a definite objective. He had said something that was dangerous and, as I saw it at the time, something that was practically impossible.

I admired him for his honesty and moral courage in admitting his conversion to the necessity of the insurrection. But most of all, I admired the logician – he was, after all, a mathematician by profession and training. It was logic that helped him see what was necessary, when so many nebulous political ideas abounded. De Valera was head and shoulders above his contemporaries (literally and metaphorically), or so I thought at that time and still do.

That idea which occurred to Dev, of designing a trench-coat, was instructive as an apt demonstration of the way his mind worked. We might have gone out marching in his trench-coat, and travelled and worked and shot at the enemy all in one day – but this idea shows, in how he then thought, that he was still in the grip of romantic ideas of the past; he had the blood of Spain mixed with the blood of Ireland in his veins. He was born in America of a Spanish father and an Irish mother. In literature and history, the Spanish are represented as both proud and romantic – there is truth in the stereotype. Indeed, with regard to so many of the leaders of the 1916 Rising, the irony further blossoms. P.H. Pearse was born of a Cornish father (Pierce) and an Irish mother, and the stereotypical Cornish are romantic in popular fiction. And even Cathal Brugha, Michael Collins' beloved antagonist, was christened Charles Burgess.

There have been apologists for Dev, who have said it was not true that he would, in the last resort, stage another 1916.

But I don't agree. To a logician and a soldier, that would have been the only alternative to a campaign of assassination. He always favoured conventional rather than guerrilla tactics.

For that next phase of the job, we would need a Mick Collins, that realist and pragmatist, who would direct fire from the very few guns left in our hands. The 1916 Rising was but an expression of the revolution, not an end. It was the first phase of our revolution, a phase now coming to an end.

★ ★ ★

Nineteen-eighteen proved eventful, and dangerous. I became part of a squad of ten men sent to London to shadow the British cabinet, and to shoot them on receipt of final orders. But the year began with more modest work on the political hustings.

During this period, a number of Volunteers had managed to get possession of small calibre revolvers, mainly .38s. In some cases, they were issued to us from our GHQ. We frequently carried the revolvers around on our persons, but very few of us realised that the logical use of them was at close range and for assassination.

On one occasion, near the Bird Cage public house in Drumcondra, the commanding officer of the 2nd Battalion, Dick McKee, was arrested in front of our eyes. A tender of police arrived on the scene. The Volunteers numbered one hundred or more, but we were told by our officers to take no action at all, and we suffered the ignominy of seeing Dick McKee surrounded by ten or twelve policemen and taken away. We were then dismissed. This (and other incidents) had a most depressing effect upon men newly recruited into our movement, and it took the heart out of the old Volunteers. I was frustrated and angry. I said bluntly at our meetings that though ill-armed, we should have resisted. The time was long past, I was convinced, for mock battle and manoeuvres; it was time again for action. For some of us, action had already begun.

There was one feature of our army that must have been unique, as a result of which an unemployed Volunteer could become a dead hero. It was the practice at a company parade to ask the unemployed men to remain after 'dismiss', and these men were detailed for duty in the daytime. They never demurred, but zealously carried out their orders. Is there anything more sublime in a revolutionary army? These men were not being paid one penny from any source or employer, yet they managed somehow to pay a few pence every week into our company's fund. It is not easy to write of it. One man I knew died in action with broken and leaky boots, and probably lacking a meal. He had refused to come to the south of Ireland with me, where a man's needs were met. He had too much pride. The Volunteers could be called many things. They could not be called mercenary.

THE SOUTH ARMAGH ELECTION

In early February of 1918, an election was contested in South Armagh by the political wing of the 'Sinn Féiners', as we were then collectively called. Though our political party at that time had no name, those returned were pledged to abstain from taking their seats in the House of Commons of the British parliament.

South Armagh was a stronghold of the parliamentary Conservative party, which had strong unionist support. Many constituents of that area were militant Orangemen, all members of a sectarian organisation, staunch supporters of continued union with Britain. This South Armagh election was, to my mind, a demonstration of the political strength and maturity of the Volunteer movement. The Orange faction was resilient and powerful in Armagh. It was considered that the Sinn Féin candidate and his agents would need some real protection.

Therefore, a large number of Volunteers from County Clare and other parts of Ireland were taken north. They marched, drilled and took up quarters in the towns and villages of South Armagh. Although there was no attempt by the Volunteers to intimidate the voters, they made it very clear that they saw themselves as a military body. I was getting my first impression of these reckless young southerners, an impression that was to last to the end.

INSIDE THE GPO

I was aide-de-camp to Michael Brennan (later General Brennan, Chief of Staff, Irish national army) at a post in a place called Forkhill. It was polling day of the election, and the polling booth was being approached by a turbulent mob of Orangemen. From their aggressive behaviour, it was obvious that they intended to attack the Sinn Féin representatives, of whom I was one.

Mick Brennan was calmly in charge, his group of Volunteers standing at ease on the roadway. The RIC were there in strength, and though they were armed and numerous, Mick pulled a bluff. He approached the RIC officer-in-charge and asked him to check the mob, which was still advancing and almost on us with assorted weapons. The RIC officer refused to make any attempt to check the mob. So Mick Brennan called on his men – mostly County Clare Volunteers – and said, 'Men with the .45s – step to the front.' To this day I remain sure that those lads were armed more with wit than weapons; but about thirty stepped to the front. As the Volunteers faced the oncoming hoard, Mick said to the RIC inspector, 'The blood will be on your head if you don't halt them.' The RIC inspector, backed by his men with carbines, immediately halted the Orange mob and then managed to disperse them. And Mick Brennan turned, grinned at me, went calmly back into his hotel, as any staff officer would – having handed over a detail to his subordinate.

The important thing about this incident is that it was then the law (and the whole country knew this) that if any man was found giving orders to civilians drawn up in military formation, that man would be promptly arrested. But Mick Brennan, who had defied the RIC and threatened them with arms, was not arrested or approached by anyone, then or later. Mick had simply gone back into his hotel, considering the incident to be closed, and the RIC inspector very clearly had no intention of disagreeing with him.

Following the election, Mick ordered me to take a column of the Clare Volunteers through Armagh, and place them on the train that ran from Dundalk to Dublin. There were about one hundred men in that column, as far as I can remember, mostly farmers' sons, obviously from a good background and full of fight. I felt I was leading a crowd of schoolboys, likely to do anything for devilment. Unfortunately, my 'schoolboys' had revolvers − I did not know how many. They did not know me, and they were enormous young countrymen. I could not help repeating in my mind the biblical phrase, 'And a little child shall lead them.'

We had barely marched out of the village of Forkhill when the first shot went off. In sheer lightheartedness, one of the men had fired his adieu to the village. I was determined that that shot would be the last one, at least while they were under my command. I halted the column. Night had fallen, and it was impossible to locate the culprit, as the gun was passed from hand to hand. I tried to trace it, and could hear them chuckling in the dark. I had a vision of myself arriving in Armagh amidst a volley of shots. It was quite a fix. But I had a lucky inspiration.

I stood them all to attention, and said to these young Claremen, 'That shot was nearly two years too late! We could have used that bullet and the gun it was fired from during Easter Week.' I drove home the point that the handiest way to avoid facing a possible enemy was to get rid of one's ammunition.

But they were fine lads – and they gave me no further trouble. They were a wild crew, and brave enough for anything. They would easily have cleared that British barricade in Moore Street in 1916, given the means. But that was the terrible thing about that whole period, from 1916 to 1921: we had only a fraction of our requirements. I thought, and still think, that in 1918 we were reaching the peak of our enthusiasm for action against the British, because in that year people of substance were giving support to and joining the Irish Volunteers. The decline that occurred later was due to our inability to arm these men adequately.

Early 1918 was a period of frustration, a period of very little activity. The Dublin Volunteers attended their parades, but it was impossible to do much foot-drill in small halls. We simply lacked competent instructors. It would have been a splendid time for all kinds of technical instruction: lectures on explosives, engineering or military tactics and history. Meanwhile, there was no advantage to be gained in making new recruits. We lacked equipment, and we were being driven underground. We had to be very circumspect in admitting new men to the movement. It is an amazing fact that the same drill halls were in use from 1917 to 1921, and were never betrayed. True, they were situated in poor districts. With the exception of the men of education who had taken part in the 1916 Rising, we gained few new men of like calibre. In China, and later in India, the university students were in the forefront of revolution. But in Dublin, they were politically inarticulate and inactive. It was still 'we few, we happy few, we band of brothers'. Why did we forget after the British left the Twenty-six Counties that we were all brothers, and could not afford to quarrel? Why did we forget all those things that should have saved us from the Civil War ... ?

THE CONSCRIPTION CRISIS

Meanwhile, the European war surged relentlessly on. Young Irishmen were adding their blood to the British blood in the mud of Flanders. But for us, the Irish Volunteers in our War of Independence, 'England's difficulty' remained, in this increasing tension, 'Ireland's opportunity'. Whenever the situation became threatening, there was a noticeable increase in our numbers on parade. This was so especially when conscription was threatened in early 1918. Though the matter was never discussed amongst us, I was alarmed. Perhaps the fact of my having been born and bred in the heart of the British Empire had something to do with this. But the more I saw of the *form* that resistance to conscription was taking, the more alarmed I became.

A kind of solemn covenant or oath was signed at church doors all over Ireland. In sermons and from the altar, congregations were exhorted to resist conscription, and the Catholic hierarchy itself made a pronouncement against it. This was followed by a pledge to resist conscription, which was signed by enormous numbers of people at church doors on the following Sunday. That pledge, I felt, would be desperately endorsed if the occasion arose; and to me that appeared terrifying. Masses of people might be led by priests to slaughter. I believed that many of the young priests would physically resist conscription but, as I saw it, the clergy in Ireland were inspiring people to a fanatical enthusiasm that they would not be able to lead or control. What was most serious, I was convinced, was that there was no word of *how* exactly conscription would be resisted.

It is easy to be wise after the event, but I was aware at the time that there was no statement by organised Labour that they would paralyse transport in the event of conscription, as they *could* have done. And even when an Irish Conscription Act *was* passed by the British government, conscription was not even discussed at my trade union meetings, and I venture to say that there exists no mention of conscription in the minutes of other trade union meetings. There appeared to be absolutely no leadership in that crisis, if we except the signing of declarations at church doors.

There was then no Dáil Éireann, and still only a very few Republican representatives (who, as elected MPs, were refusing to take their seats in Whitehall). So it was clear to me that we had no means of resistance except armed action – an armed action that could be strategic, limited, but effective. Such as a successful attack on the British cabinet.

Volunteer GHQ had a moral responsibility for what would ensue if conscription were resisted by force of arms, even if we had little to fight with. I still believe that during that crisis, no Volunteer should have allowed himself to be arrested if he possessed or had access to arms.

As I saw it, force could only be met by force. Conflict was inevitable. It was only a matter of who would fire first, and our moral position could only be reinforced if we were the first to take the field. It was suggested then that the British government intended imposing conscription in Ireland to crush Sinn Féin. This was my own view, since I was born and brought up in London. Irish-born people did not understand that Englishmen regarded Irishmen as fellow-Britishers, somewhat rowdy, but good fellows when disciplined; believed that Englishmen were protecting the Irish from

German aggression; that only a few misguided Irishmen had stabbed them in the back in 1916; and that 'German gold' was sustaining Sinn Féin.

I had some contact with political thought in Britain. The more liberal politicians in England had no idea of the scale of our national resurgence. The Scots had been silent since the Battle of Flodden, and the Welsh hadn't been in revolt since the Middle Ages. Responsible British statesmen had no concept of that new Irish resurgence, or even of the strength of the literary renaissance launched by Yeats and other writers. It was not part of their own history or experience.

Certainly, the political, religious and literary renaissance under the Tudors, the English Civil War of 1642–49, and the restoration of Charles II in England, had been anything but a people's movement. And some members of the current British cabinet would quite willingly have carried out dragooning in Ireland. Bonar Law (a most dangerous man) was certainly prepared to enforce conscription in Ireland. F.E. Smith was another dangerous man; and General Wilson, subsequently the commander-in-chief of British forces in Ireland, who was hand-in-glove with Lloyd George, stated that he could handle recalcitrant Irishmen. Wilson said publicly that he 'would deal with 300,000 bolshie Irishmen – with pleasure'. General Haig's back was really to the wall in France. I knew this much, if little else.

In free time from my electrician's work, I scouted around the environs of Dublin and the surrounding countryside. I looked into the railway yards, and saw what appeared to be excessively large amounts of railway sleepers – often newly milled timber. This reminded me of that military barricade I had encountered at the top of Moore Street in 1916. The British had piled up those railway sleepers before which The O'Rahilly had died. Railway sleepers provided the ideal barricade. With such massive barricades, any area throughout all of Ireland might be sealed off with ease, and those within the enclosure could be rounded up effortlessly.

This was the situation in April 1918, when I was working in a shell factory in Parkgate Street, Dublin. A number of other Irish Volunteers worked there, including Sam Reilly, Matt Furlong and the toughest nut of all – Joe Leonard. That April, I took a holiday from that factory, where I was working as an electrician. Illogical, perhaps, to be making munitions for one's enemy.

Patriotism only sustains one in fits and starts. During 1918 in Ireland, the Volunteers were no more illogical than the pro-British minority in Ireland – who prayed for a British victory, and yet secretly hoped that the Irish revolutionaries would save them from implementing their avowed loyalty by serving in the British forces. It was a policy of ours in that factory to get the greatest possible amount of wages while doing the least possible amount of work – without getting ourselves sacked.

INSIDE THE GPO

My week's holiday, with the addition of two Sundays at the beginning and end, meant that I could take a quick look around the south and a bit of the western counties. I was now committed to finding out if the British were in earnest about enforcing conscription. If they were, there would be signs of military preparation. And there *were* such signs: an obvious abundance of sandbags and material for barricades. The idea was simple. Each village or town would be cut off and dealt with, piecemeal. Pledges against conscription would be of little avail against British troops still sore at the 1916 'stab-in-the-back'.

I travelled through a good deal of the country, ending my trip in the west when I reached the Irish-speaking Gaeltacht. There were three things of particular interest.

The first thing I observed was that the people were very polite to the RIC. Too polite, I thought. They said 'Sir', and dusted their chairs for the 'Peeler' – as policemen in Ireland were then still called. The second thing I noticed was that de Valera was popular; his photograph was in the place of honour in many houses. I was surprised at this, for he was not long out of jail, but the feeling went deep for Dev in that part of Mayo. There was some unique quality in the attitude of people towards Dev. True, he had made the best fight of all the Dublin commandants in 1916 – but what the people felt for him was a form of reverence. Was it because of the old prophecy of Columcille, that 'A Spaniard would free Ireland'? Or do peasants recognise a man with a mission before other people do? I never approved of Carlyle's heroes and hero-worship — but here was one of Carlyle's imponderables.

The third thing that I noticed was the presence, everywhere and on a vast scale, of those unexpected quantities of railway sleepers, and far more than could be contemplated for regular railway maintenance. They could only be intended for use in making barricades to isolate the towns and villages while the men were being rounded up for service. It was clearly a British military objective. I was as sure that this was so as if I had intercepted their operational dispatches.

On my return to Dublin at the end of my ten-day journey, I was to report on all of this to Mick Collins. He had been arrested for making a speech. He had been given bail and then had broken it. Tension was mounting.

I was convinced that conscription, if applied in Ireland, would be similar to the events preceding Cromwell's Irish campaign: an insurrection of a sort had preceded that bloodiest of conquests. Our Volunteers were not strong enough to fight a defensive war, but were sufficiently enthusiastic to lead us into plenty of bloodshed.

It was a grave situation. I don't know how any Irishman with a sense of responsibility could have been unaware of it, though some of the Volunteers, especially those from England, were aware of this danger. I was wondering if the British cabinet could be intimidated. One member of that cabinet, the Welshman Lloyd George, was not without vision. Though the conscription part of the act was already passed in parliament, it would not be operative until an 'order in council' was signed by members of that cabinet. Perhaps if some of their cabinet were shot, the British government could be ... impressed.

Two things I believed: that a determined man cannot be halted – he will get there; secondly, that even a brave man can be deterred from a doubtful experiment if it means the loss of his life. I did not know if I could be placed in that first category. However, 'It's polite to wait till you're asked' – as people say in Ireland.

Above: A sketch of the scene inside the GPO during the Rising.

Below: The mangled interior of the GPO after the insurrection.

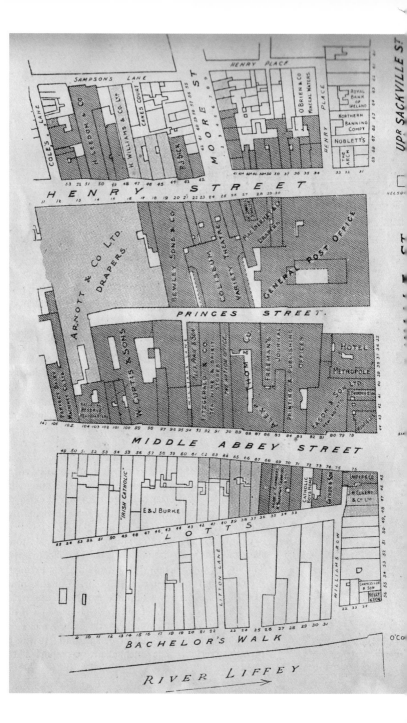

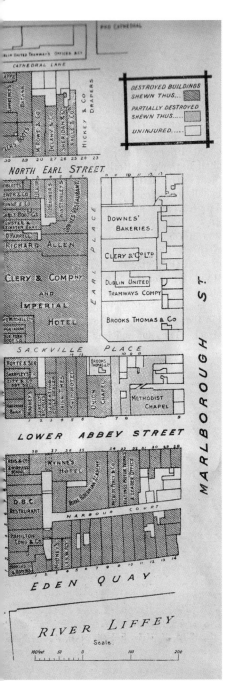

A map of the destruction wrought in the immediate proximity of the GPO. Good initially held Kelly and Son's gun shop, marked at the corner of Lower Sackville Street and Bachelor's Walk. After abandoning the GPO, the rebels crossed Henry Street into Henry Place, at the top centre of the map.

Above: Dublin citizens inspect the carnage in the wake of the Rising.

After the Insurrection.—
Corner of Bachelor's Walk and Lr. Sackville Street
which commanded O'Connell Bridge.

Left: The ruins of Kelly's gun shop, on the corner of Bachelor's Walk, after the Rising.

Óglaigh na hÉireann belt buckle and crossed bayonets.

In order to prevent the further slaughter of Dublin citizens, and in the hope of saving the lives of our followers now surrounded and hopelessly outnumbered, the members of the Provisional Government present at Head-Quarters have agreed to an unconditional surrender, and the Commandants of the various districts in the City and Country will order their commands to lay down arms.

P. H. Pearse

29th April 1916

3.45 p.m.

I agree to these conditions for the men only under my own Command in the Moore Street District and for the men in the Stephen's Green Command.

James Connolly

April 29/16

On consultation with Commandant Ceannt and other officers I have decided to agree to unconditional surrender also.

Thomas MacDonagh.

'In order to prevent the further slaughter of Dublin citizens ...'
The surrender order, signed by PH Pearse, James Connolly and
Thomas MacDonagh, 29 April 1916.

Patrick Pearse surrendering to General Lowe and his son John.
Elizabeth O'Farrell's dress and boots are clearly visible.

Above: Prisoners being marched towards the docks for transportation to British prisons.

Left: Kerryman Thomas Ashe, who led the 5th Battalion in 1916. Ashe died in 1917 after being force fed whilst on hunger strike.

LONDON REVISITED

ON MY RETURN from the south and west, I was called up to our GHQ on an evening in mid-April. I went to our GHQ in Parnell Square, and saw in the hall there a Volunteer whom I knew well from London. It was my old friend Bill Whelan. He told me that he had a suspicion of what he had been called up for, and asked me, 'What are *you* here for?'

I was noncommittal at first, but then admitted, 'I have a good idea. Haven't you?' And he said, 'Yes.'

When I entered that room, I saw two men, Cathal Brugha and Dick Mulcahy. They both sat at separate green baize-covered card tables. There was no one else in the room. Cathal Brugha said immediately to me, 'You have been recommended as one likely to go on a dangerous mission. It is of such a nature that provision will be made for your dependants, if any.'

I replied that I had 'already considered' such a mission, and that it was 'only a matter of who would bell the cat', and that, alas, I 'knew the terrain – so to speak'.

They were both silent for a moment, and then Cathal Brugha asked me who I had been speaking to. I replied that I had been speaking to no one, but that I had been thinking the matter over for some time.

Brugha then said to me, '*What* have you been thinking of?'

I told him, 'I was thinking that the British cabinet might be deterred if some of them are shot.'

There was a silence in the room. Mulcahy and Brugha then told me to consider the matter, and if I was of the same mind I was to report in a week, naming a precise time and date. I passed Bill Whelan on the way out and nodded to him – as if to say, you have guessed right.

My trade union was a few doors distant, so I decided to pay my arrears – some three pounds odd. A meeting was in progress, and I sat beside a Volunteer with whom I was very intimate. I'd always thought he knew more about things political than I did. He asked me why I had been called to GHQ, and I replied by tightening my tie. It was clear that he understood me. It transpired that he, who was also a Londoner, was considered too well known to go there on the mission that was being planned. It turned out that we had both recommended each other for that same mission.

Bill Whelan and I went to GHQ a week later, and were asked if we had considered the matter. We were told that it was proposed to shoot members of the British government, and thus prevent their signing the order-in-council that would make the application for conscription in Ireland operative. We were given a number of addresses in London where our party would stay, two men at each address. Either Dick Mulcahy or Cathal Brugha had a list of Dublin addresses, which was shown to Whelan and me. We were asked if we frequented any of them. We were ordered to avoid any of those places, because many of them would soon be raided by British intelligence.

Cathal Brugha then asked us if we had our 'arrangements made', meaning had we made arrangements for our relatives or dependants. He then assured us that our families would be sustained. We were each given five pounds. Cathal told us to take the Holyhead boat and go by train from there to Euston Station in London. He then concluded our meeting by saying, 'I will be with you and in charge of the party. I will take advice or instructions from no one, unless I request it – is that understood?'

I had a good look at Cathal Brugha, and decided that he was not a man one would argue with. I had never seen a more grim man – or one with, often, such merry eyes. He would stop at nothing, but would always spare a comrade, if possible. He was one of the few men I've ever met who knew his mind; a lover of his fellow men, absolutely ruthless in action, and, in our movement, the 'noblest Roman of them all'.

Cathal Brugha and Michael Collins were brilliant partners. Closest of friends, both were known for taking enormous risks. They were later on opposing sides in the Civil War. Brugha would die with two .45 Colts blazing, one in each hand like a figure in North American myth, but in his native city of Dublin, where he had suffered more than thirty wounds during the Rising of Easter week. Collins died in an ambush only a stone's throw from his own town of Clonakilty in County Cork. It was a savage irony that two such noble men should die so soon afterwards, on opposing sides in the tragic Civil War ...

Within a few days, Bill Whelan and I went to London. Bill left a letter for his mother. Strange how the hardest cases have a last thought for their mothers; it was the only touch of sentiment I ever saw in Bill. Most of my own family were still living in London, but, for reasons of security, I was not able to contact any of them during this time.

We travelled saloon class via Holyhead. Bill fell asleep beside me on a deck-chair. A detective approached, scrutinising faces closely. I nudged Bill and whispered a warning. There was a possibility he might be recognised. I have never seen a man react so quickly. Bill made a wild dive in the direction of the detective – as if about to vomit. The detective had seen enough of that – it was a rough crossing – and retired very promptly.

We got to London without further incident. We had a poor breakfast in London because of food rationing, and we had no ration cards. When we read the morning papers, we were dismayed to learn that a large number of Irish political leaders, including de Valera, had just been arrested. We were anxious about Cathal Brugha. We knew he would fight for his liberty and, as there was no news of any shooting incident, we concluded that he had escaped the round-up.

After breakfast, we made a tour of the London addresses that had been given to us before we left Dublin, as places where our party were to be housed. There were ten men in all in our unit, two to each house. 'The Skipper', as we called Cathal, had his own arrangement.

At every address except one that Bill Whelan and I visited, there was no one in residence. We got no answer at any of these doors. The occupants had flown – no doubt they would come back on the trade winds, I thought. At one place, we were informed that the lady of the house had gone to Ireland, though her husband remained. I knew that these people had been told by Jack Nunan of our coming, and that they had consented to harbour us. I told the man of this last house that I would billet two men on him, and this I did. The two men were Sammy Reilly and Matt Furlong. But in order to arrange further accommodations, I was having to make use of my personal or family contacts.

I had one address in London that was to be used only as a last resort. It was situated in the East End of London, and was possibly under suspicion. The name of the people was O'Connor. Eventually I had to visit this house, where I found six men had arrived, and all of them were armed. This was a small house, and in wartime London even one able-bodied young man in a household was conspicuous – let alone six men. So Bill Whelan and I made a hurried tour of London-Irish families, and secured lodgings for two men in other houses. Three of these families had sons who had taken part in the insurrection, and were therefore not considered safe from enemy surveillance, but we had no further choice. The family with whom Bill Whelan and I stayed probably guessed that they risked severe sentences for harbouring us, but we were made welcome, and fed on their limited rations, as we still had no ration cards. I cannot speak too highly of the courage, hospitality and kindness of the people who harboured us.

Cathal Brugha stayed in a large house, with his daughter, a very young child, near Tavistock Place, not far from Regent's Park. An Irishwoman, Mrs Sean McGrath, acted as a kind of housekeeper and went to the house daily, but – with the exception of his young daughter – Cathal Brugha lived apart.

Bill Whelan, Matt Furlong and I visited Cathal Brugha several times, and he made some attempt to entertain us. He had a large number of photographs of political celebrities, members of the British cabinet and important newspaper men – Northcliffe and some others. He seemed to get the greatest pleasure out of discussing these people; much the same as some people look at photographs of film stars. After discussing these people for some time one evening, I suggested we talk about the spring, or Kew Gardens in lilac-time. On leaving Brugha with his small daughter that night, I said to Bill, 'It was the Schooner Hesperus that sailed the stormy seas!'

'I know,' said Bill. 'It is very sad, but he's wise to keep us at a distance.'

Around about that time, I'd begun to be aware of a fascinating connection, a common factor shared by men like Cathal and P.H. Pearse, and even de Valera. They all had Irish mothers. Perhaps, because they were half-Irish, a tension bred from their mixed origins made them all zealots. Cathal Brugha's name was a gaelicised rendering of Charles Burgess; I believe his father was a Yorkshireman. And Patrick 'Pierce' (a Cornish surname) had become Padraig Pearse; or Padraig MacPiarish, as befitted the author of the Proclamation of 1916. And the half-Spanish de Valera (Dev to generations to come) had the Irish Christian name of Eamon. All three of them were essentially lonely men, and shared a kind of austerity, which harmonised interestingly with their gentle manner.

I remarked to Bill Whelan on Cathal Brugha's deliberate and maintained isolation, and Bill agreed that it was obviously to keep us at a healthy distance. There was one man amongst us with whom he was in closer contact, and this was Matt Furlong. In this I consider Cathal Brugha was a good judge. I would say that Matt Furlong − as he had proved so often with Mick Collins − was the best man (excluding Brugha himself) on that mission.

We managed to get Cathal to Kew Gardens on one occasion, and rowing on the Thames with us − and we very nearly tumbled him into the river. We were passing through a lock and there was some rough water. Cathal was sitting in the bow when we gave the boat a sudden push and it struck the water hard. We had forgotten that Cathal was not yet completely healed of his wounds − of which he had many − and we were shamefaced when we remembered, but he laughed at us and put us at our ease.

He had decided that the time had come when he must meet us all together − all ten of us in the same place. It would have been unwise for all of us to gather at his address and, knowing how well I knew London, Cathal consulted me as to where we might meet and be least conspicuous. I suggested a rendezvous in Regent's Park, where we could all be scattered and yet see him and approach individually.

Our meeting was arranged, and Cathal arrived promptly on time, but I gasped when he came riding his bicycle along the paths as if he were in Dublin's Phoenix Park, in which there are some roads open to traffic. He passed a policeman. At that period, one was not even allowed to wheel a bike through Regent's Park. The policeman stopped him and was obviously informing him of his error. Cathal seemed to be chatting to the policeman calmly enough. It was ludicrous. Trivial things always seemed to happen on the most desperate occasions. Cathal went on chatting to the policeman. I said to Bill Whelan, 'What do we do if the policeman should arrest Brugha?' and Bill, who now had his gun in his lap, replied, 'We'll soon find out.'

Cathal continued conversing in great ease with the policeman. He was evidently discovering the surprise he must have caused and receiving some admonishment for cycling within the genteel precincts of Regent's Park. We waited. The rest of our group, spread out within close reach, waited also.

Eventually, the policeman let Cathal go, and moved on. Cathal then sat on a bench, and after a little while we approached him one by one. He told us that the attack plan was made; that we would each be assigned a member of the cabinet. One name of a member of the cabinet would be drawn at a time from a hat, and allotted to one of us. We would maintain surveillance of the man whose name had been picked at random, and, on our final orders, we would execute him. Matt Furlong would bring those final orders.

'That is all for this day,' Cathal told each of us in turn, and we then dispersed. I was tempted to ask Cathal what he had to talk about to that policeman that took so long, but I'd heard enough for one day.

There were eleven of us in all at that meeting in Regent's Park: Cathal Brugha, Matt Furlong, Martin Gleeson, Sam Reilly, James 'Ginger' McNamara, Tom Craven, Bill Whelan, Peter Murtagh, James Mooney, myself, and I forget the other. By a strange coincidence, a lady whom I met later that same day said to me, 'I saw a Dublin man near Regent's Park, walking along the road. He had cycle clips on his trousers and a cycle-pump in his hand ... Now, wasn't that a Dublin man?'

She had obviously seen Cathal Brugha as he was walking through the streets, which shows how very easily he could have been picked up. The description she gave me was a mode of behaviour and appearance peculiar to Dublin, but very rare in London. I would have liked to point this out to Cathal. But I did not.

While we waited for orders throughout the weeks that followed, there were frequent periods during which we were advised that we were 'off duty' for a limited time, usually on weekends or on public holidays. It struck me that these would have been the optimum chances for attack. But I held my own counsel.

To make use of those 'holidays', I introduced the lads to sculling, and we spent some of the time on the River Lea.

Although we could not get a great deal of food, I considered we should get plenty of exercise, so we would go sculling or rowing in pairs. On returning one day from this exercise, I was told that the 'lottery' had been made; that the names had been picked from a hat, and that I had got Bonar Law.

I remembered saying to Cathal Brugha in Dublin, when he told us that others as well as the cabinet members might be shot, 'I'm for the cabinet,' a remark which was repeated by Bill Whelan. Cathal had looked sternly at us and then smiled. So Bill and I had been given two of the 'favourites'. One wondered about the hand that had picked the names from the hat.

I had nothing against Bonar Law, except that he was fond of matinees. We were to be often at the theatre together, and I got to know his habits well, though he, of course, was unaware of the existence of his escort. And I was many times close to Bonar Law's heels as he walked from Downing Street to the Houses of Parliament. It seemed to me that he was singularly incautious, considering all that he had done and proposed to do in Ireland. It seemed that he had no sixth sense. He could not have had the experience of living dangerously. It's surprising how safe public figures in England felt then.

From day to day, we expected our orders to attack. It was very wearing. Matt Furlong would appear suddenly when we were sitting at a meal, and we would hurry away – only to be told it was postponed again. Every day, Bill used to hold his gun in his hand and sight it to see whether it shook, and then say, 'So far, so good,' when he found his hand remained steady.

After a sudden visit from Matt on one occasion, I said to Bill, 'Do you find that it gets into everything, what you eat and what you drink?' and he replied, 'Everything.' For my part, when I was first considering the matter back in Dublin, I thought it unfortunate that one should die loving the world so much and those in it, and that it was a pity people did not know how much I liked them. I sometimes thought of what the world was going to lose when I would be killed. I knew I would become useless and maudlin if I continued in this vein, so I deliberately engaged in violent exercise, with the result that I slept well. So did Bill Whelan, though he took things easily, at least physically. Each to his own method of relaxation – whatever works best. I did not know what went on in his mind, of course, except that – like me – he was quite swollen-headed at being amongst the first to be picked for this operation. We both slept like babes. We had something else in common: it was knowing that many things are planned and few are executed, and that the actual execution would bear little relation to the agreed plan.

Then, as the weeks went by and became months, the enemy did not follow up the earlier arrests of our leaders by putting conscription into immediate effect. Our Volunteer GHQ staff was at liberty, and Collins just could not be caught. Yet there seemed no explanation for why the British should delay implementing the act.

Cathal Brugha was very anxious to get on with the job, and sent Matt Furlong to Dublin on several occasions, pressing for consent to commence operations.

There was one point that I thought rather unrealistic. We were nearly all armed with .38 revolvers. A .38 is not at all a deadly weapon, unless you are lucky and several shots can be fired. Cathal, I well knew, possessed superior armament, having a heavy automatic pistol with long range, the one that was then known as a 'Peter-the-Painter'. Still, I had plenty of ammunition – about fifty rounds.

In our lodgings in London, it was not easy for us to avoid eating meals for which we were not paying. This troubled us all. Bill Whelan and I endeavoured to 'dine out' whenever possible. But in the cafes or restaurants, one could only get one egg per meal. One stunt we worked was to order one egg and toast, eat this, leave the table and return for another. But we could only get scrap meals, and with all the sculling we were losing weight. And, in any event, Matt Furlong kept turning up and spoiling our appetites. We would act tomorrow, he'd tell us; or tomorrow. Or tomorrow.

Then, one day, I left the house for only a short time and missed the big moment. Matt came to the house and took Bill with him, though they had left a message for me to 'stay put' in Ernie Nunan's, where we were staying.

That evening when Bill got back, he said to me, 'You missed it!'

'Missed what?'

'We had a rendezvous in the House of Commons. Cathal wanted to test the possibilities. He took Matt and me into the gallery.'

'Of the House of Commons?'

'That's right.'

'How did you get in?'

'We got in on Ginnell's ticket.'

Ginnell was a sympathetic MP in the Irish parliamentary party: he'd been the only member of that party to raise a voice in protest at the executions after Easter week in 1916.

'So,' I said, 'you got in ... Were there many members in the House?'

'Packed,' said Bill with a grin. 'Bonar Law was speaking.'

'Bonar Law ... You mean my chap?'

'Yes,' replied Bill, 'and Cathal stood up to get a good look at him – and leaned over the gallery.'

'Did he get a good look?'

'Not exactly – Bonar Law was out of sight and underneath us. Cathal could not possibly have hit him from his position in the gallery.'

'You mean Cathal was armed?'

'Well, we were *all* armed,' said Bill. 'In fact, Cathal had his "Peter-the-Painter" underneath his coat. We were sitting beside him, one on each side, Matt and I. An usher approached us and told Cathal "not to stand up or look over the gallery"!'

'And the House was nearly full of members?'

'Oh, yes, it was really crowded,' said Bill, 'but mostly by members who were in uniform.'

'Well,' I said, 'at least you'd have been firing at soldiers.'

'A pity you missed it,' said Bill.

True: if that had been the time, I would have missed it.

★ ★ ★

There were at least two occasions shortly after that when Bill Whelan and I were told to parade at Downing Street, and were informed that our targets would be coming out of Downing Street, that this was our part of the operation – but at the last moment we were told again, 'Not today.'

By some extraordinary luck, we were never accosted in London. On one occasion, Bill and I were leaving a picture-house. Police were questioning those leaving. We gave our Dublin addresses, and were not delayed. Four of the ten men of our party in London, including myself, were actually liable for conscription. It seemed to me then (as it often has since) that there was an extraordinary naiveté about us *and* them – both gunmen and the then British authorities!

INSIDE THE GPO

Occasionally, while walking through the streets, we saw a deserter with his escorts; it never occurred to us that we might be challenged ourselves. We were always armed, but it is very doubtful that we would have escaped if forced into action. On one occasion, six of us met accidentally in Victoria Street, within 200 yards of the House of Commons! We all laughed outright.

There were occasional German bombing raids during this period, between May and August. Londoners, as far as I could judge, were not seriously disturbed during the air raids, but I think it got on the nerves of some of our men. I had experienced Zeppelin raiding before, and was not so disturbed, because I was in my home town. For a long while, I ignored a thought I'd had, which was triggered by air raids. In fact, I deliberately refused to think about the matter. At last, one night, during a raid, I said to Bill Whelan, 'Here's a chance to do the job – the perfect chance. We should do it while they are in their cellars.' I told Bill that I was going to go to Cathal Brugha to put this up to him. Bill restrained me from doing so, and I can imagine now what answer I would have got from Cathal Brugha. He was not the man to put up with suggestions.

But at that time, I was thinking of doing the job with some real chance of saving my own life. Absolutely the wrong attitude, of course, if anything of this sort was to be successful. When the time arrived, it had to be done without regard to cost, or it would never be done at all.

Some of the lads of our party must have been cracking up, because I heard afterwards that two of them were praying hard for themselves during a raid, instead of praying for more raids, as was logical. But I'd experienced bombing before, and was on my own dunghill. In thinking back now, I can see that those Zeppelin raids of 1918 were mere pinpricks, compared with those of the Blitz of London in World War II.

Once, we were at a theatre, seeing a play called *The Knife*, when bombing began. The raid was very close, and the audience stood up to leave. We were in an expensive part of the house, and until the bombing began, we had both found the play very flat and in somewhat bad taste, but now found it rather thrilling, and I got a certain amount of pleasure in saying, 'Hush – Hush!' – as if anxious to hear the actors. This had a certain calming effect, the English being quick to remember their traditional phlegm. We had one thrill that night ourselves, as Bill had left his coat in the cloakroom with his gun still in the pocket, but we recovered it without incident.

Bonar Law and I went to the opera a good deal, though it was hardly the operatic season, I believe. One night, Bill and I were standing on the balcony of a theatre that then existed near Oxford Circus; we were blowing any spare cash we had – for 'the time had come, the walrus said'! The orders were that it would be 'definitely tomorrow'.

Bill was looking down into the street at the civilians, and at the newsboys diving between the traffic. He was silent for a long time. I said to him, 'What are you looking at?'

And he said, 'I'm thinking some of those poor bloody kids could be killed tomorrow.' But it was another 'much ado about nothing'; the action was postponed yet again.

For a long time, I succeeded in ignoring the whole business by saying to myself, 'The longer it is put off, the better,' or, 'This thing – could last a lifetime.' Having known a series of long, anxious periods in my life, I refused to conjecture on the matter, but it got to me at last. I was anxious to get it over with – whichever way it might turn out. And still thought that the job should be done, willy-nilly, during the next air raid.

Eventually, sometime in August, a few of our lads were sent home. The British position in France was improving, and that may have been the reason, since it meant that conscription in Ireland was less likely. Bill and Sam and I were the last to leave, except for Brugha, and Matt Furlong, who I believe stayed in London. I never saw Matt alive again. He was killed, I think in 1920.[46] Matt carried that fatal look in his face, I thought. He was the gentlest amongst us.

---

46 He died on 15 October 1920, from injuries received while testing munitions in Dunboyne, County Meath.

PASSAGE BACK TO DUBLIN

Bill Whelan and I went to Liverpool, and were there about a fortnight, trying to arrange a free passage home. During most of that time, we had no money at all, but lodged with several sympathisers. It was easier to find staunch supporters in Liverpool, easier than in any other part of England. Liverpool people were very obviously not at all afraid of associating with active Volunteers. The Irish who had gone to London and settled there were, to a great extent, now civil servants, teachers or people in the more lucrative jobs.

Something wonderful happened to us in Liverpool, which was a demonstration of the character of the common people of that city. The Liverpool Irish had sent much the largest contingent to take part in 1916. The poorest in the famine years had managed only to reach Liverpool; fidelity to Ireland appeared to be inversely proportionate to the fare home.

What happened to Bill and myself there was charming. We were, as I've said, totally without funds. A working man, Neil Kerr, gave us an envelope containing money, and told us that he had been ordered to give it to us. But that story was too thin. We were tradesmen ourselves, and recognised a tradesman's pay packet. His name had been erased, and Neil Kerr swore he had been told to give it to us. It was impossible to convince our experienced eyes, and we left the pay package with him. But he slipped it again into my coat pocket later. Neil Kerr was old enough to be a father to either of us. He was a stevedore.[47]

Eventually we were informed that we would be able to get a boat to Dublin, but that we would have to stow away on it. We were obliged to stow away because, just as we were about to leave, Delia Larkin arrived from America, and we understood that she carried a large sum of money raised there for Sinn Féin. She got the berth on the boat, which had to be paid for with the money for our passage, and we were to be hidden in the fo'c's'le. We were not particularly pleased when we had to wait for yet another ship.

But at last we were stowed away in the fo'c's'le of a Guinness boat bound for Dublin. I hid in one seaman's bunk, and Bill in a second one on the opposite side of the companionway. Shortly after leaving the docks, a sailor came below and sat on the edge of my bunk – and then lay back across my body. I decided to remain perfectly still. After a while, the sailor sat up suddenly and spoke to another seaman, saying he thought he had fleas, and started to curse, saying that he'd done his best to 'rid the fo'c's'le of these ruddy fleas'! Then he laid down across my body again.

---

47 Neil Kerr, in fact a purser on a shipping line, was IRB Head Centre for Liverpool, and Collins' agent. He probably was acting on orders.

Bill, meanwhile, was opposite me in the dark fo'c's'le. Occasionally, he wiped sweat from his face, put a naggin bottle of whiskey to his lips, and made a motion each time of drinking to my health. I lay very still, but was beginning to imagine fleas. Another seaman came down into the fo'c's'le and said to my incumbent, 'Get up – you are lying on a man.' The poor devil jumped to his feet as if he had been shot: a pal of his (who had previously occupied that bunk) was already long dead and buried in Liverpool.

When we got within sight of Lambay Island before entering Dublin harbour, Bill said to me, 'There it is. Did you ever think you would see it again?' We were back in Ireland. Neither of us had thought we would ever see it again. I felt pleased, but my pleasure was of a different quality. To him it was his mother, his home, his very being. To me it was something different: a somewhat provincial city, where a few men dwelt whom we called comrades, and whom we knew we could trust, those few who were the 'music makers, the dreamers of dreams'.[48] Somewhere, behind them perhaps, existed the substance of the dream. I had not yet seen it, though I had sensed it in the poems of James Clarence Mangan and Thomas Davis. But where was the fuel of the deep emotional fire from which came the flame that claimed victim after victim? Maybe I would find it further inland?

---

48 Arthur O'Shaughnessy, 'Ode'.

INSIDE THE GPO

Beyond Dublin lay Ireland. I had seen only a little of it so far, and I now decided to see and know much more of the country. I had grown critical, as one is apt to become, overnight, at the age of twenty-three. And I'd been at very full stretch, emotionally and imaginatively, for four or five months.

WITH MICHAEL COLLINS AGAIN

WHEN BILL WHELAN and I arrived in Dublin, we had to face more everyday facts. Bill took me to his home, where I stayed that first night. Having no money, I was not inclined to return to my old digs in Eccles Street, although I am sure I would have been welcomed.

The following day, Bill and I tried to contact someone who could tell us where we might get in touch with some of our senior officers or political leaders. We were informed in most cases that 'so and so' was on the run. Everyone, it seemed, was on the run. After many more inquiries, we became irritated, for it appeared to us that some sort of panic had ensued in Dublin after the earlier mass arrests that had occurred while we were in London.

Most of us who had been on the London mission had disposed of our worldly goods. Both Bill and I had actually left our tools, for anyone to take, at the jobs on which we had been working, thinking we would have no further use for them. Bill was a carpenter, and I was an electrician. We got the impression that it was regarded as almost indecent to inquire about those who were 'On The Run' – as if being 'ON THE RUN' were the most irrefutable proof of revolutionary fervour. We thought otherwise.

We met Peter Murtagh, one of our party who had been to London. He was back in his job as manager of a picture-house, and he told us that James Mooney, another of our London party, was walking the streets without employment or means of support. This information made Bill Whelan and me very angry. We had expected, in our vanity, to be received as two saved from the burning, and we were still feeling conceited that we had been chosen from so many for such a dangerous mission.

The main office of the New Ireland Insurance Company then occupied only the second floor of Kapp and Petersen's (pipe-makers and tobacconists), site of my first outpost in 1916 on Bachelor's Walk.[49] It was Bill Whelan's idea, I think, that we might find succour there; we were sure to know someone sympathetic to the cause in charge – or so we thought at the time.

Just before going to London, I had called at that same office and tried to take out a life insurance policy for a

---

49 Formerly Kelly's Gun Shop.

hundred pounds – hoping that my mother would receive it in the event of my death. Michael Staines, who was in charge of the New Ireland Insurance office at that time, had refused to give me such a policy, so I had concluded that he was 'in-the-know' about my prospects of survival. If still around, he'd be qualified to help us.

Bill and I entered the New Ireland Insurance offices, and Michael Staines was there, alone. In answer to our enquiries, however, he told us that he did not know where anyone was! We explained our position, and asked him for money. He assured us that he had none except his own, and gave us a few shillings.

Outside the GPO, historic site of revolution, which we'd now passed a dozen or so times on our quest for anyone connected with things revolutionary, we at last encountered ex-Major General Bob Price, who told us that he had just returned from the country, where he had been organising, and that we would find Mick Collins at Lynch's house in Richmond Road.

★ ★ ★

Mick Collins' epitaph should have read, 'He Was Always and Ever Available'. Joe Leonard, I believe, coined this expression, and Joe Leonard should have known.

Bill Whelan and I went to that house in Drumcondra,

where we'd been told that Collins was staying. By now we'd become certain, at long last, that we were finally headed in the right direction. If anyone could help us, it would be Mick. If anyone still needed us, it would be Mick. And if anything was still happening, Mick would be the one responsible for it happening. When we got to the house in Richmond Road, we went up the stairs two at a time and entered Mick's room very quickly.

As we opened the door, Mick was sweeping papers off his table towards a fire, but he stopped when he recognised us and cursed at us, and we cursed back. First, there was a tirade between Bill and Mick, and then a storm between Mick and myself, gaining momentum as it went along, until Mick shouted, 'What the bloody hell is it you want, anyway?'

'Money!' I answered.

'How much?' roared Mick.

'Five pounds,' I replied, 'for tools and a week's digs.'

'And yourself?' said Mick to Bill Whelan.

'Five pounds would be fair enough,' replied Bill, 'for about five months' hard labour in London.'

'I suppose that's reasonable,' said Mick.

'You're damned right it's reasonable,' I said.

We then explained that four of our party were mechanics, one a tool-maker, one a fitter and one an electrician. And that one of our party, James Mooney – to whom I have already referred – had finished his time in a furnishing establishment, Messrs Pim and Co., and was not allowed to resume his job.

'Victimised?' asked Mick.

'That's damn right,' I said.

'So,' said Mick, 'that's what all this excitement is about.'

'There's more,' I replied.

And I told him that I had met a man who had been with our party in London; that he was three weeks back in Dublin, was out of a job and had no place to live.

'That little ...' began Mick, and the row started all over again.

'He went where *you* bloody well *sent* him!' I said.

There was a pause. Mick grinned, and said, 'What you need is some action.'

At which we all roared laughing.

'Look here,' said Collins to us both, 'Mick Lynch is coming out of jail tomorrow. Don't let him be arrested again.'

He gave Bill Whelan and me a gun apiece, and told us we would find two parties of Volunteers, and that we were to divide up the Volunteers between us if it were necessary to receive support in the course of the operation.

Michael Collins then called me aside, as if to whisper in my ear, and then gave me a sharp pinch on the ear with his teeth. I had taught him that trick once, when we'd been wrestling in Frongoch Camp – though I remember reading since then that Napoleon had a trick of pinching ears.

INSIDE THE GPO

The following morning, Bill Whelan and I went to
Mountjoy Goal. Detectives from the British Special Branch,
backed by policemen, were standing at the gates, and we
spoke to them. We had already placed our supports – ten
Volunteers in two sections, both in the immediate vicinity.
They were, like us, ten out-of-work men; one was a cripple.

On his release, Mick Lynch came out of the gate and got
into a waiting car. No attempt was made to rearrest him.
I went over to the car and dropped my gun through the
window and walked away. I was sick of it all.

I believed that this military play-acting would not get us
anywhere, and our so-called 'politicians' were far too readily
scattered. I thought that something like a Janissary Guard[50]
was essential to the Irish people, for the British had fits of
legislative lunacy, which drove our people to desperation
every now and again.

I thought Michael Collins was heroic and pitiable; that he
was foolishly trying to maintain, on his own, the resistance
to conscription, whilst others were allowing themselves to
be arrested. He was trying to rescue arrested Volunteers, by
force of arms if necessary. His GHQ were intact, and they
were loyal comrades, but Collins was the only one of the
political leaders who, in my opinion, was a practical revolutionary. Always available, his instructions – and the means
to carry out those instructions – were given in meticulous

50 Bodyguard and standing army of the Turkish sultan from 1330 to 1826.

detail. Mick had one great advantage over all of his contemporaries; he knew the English and their art of dissimulation – could even beat them at that game. And he had the common touch.

Soon after what was to prove one of my last meetings with Mick Collins, I had an accident. I wrote to Mick later and asked him for a personal loan of ten pounds, impressing upon him that I meant it personally. Michael Collins sent me this money immediately. I never had a chance to repay it.

TO THE END OF 1918

I resumed work for a time in the same shell factory where I'd been employed before going to London. Joe Leonard had also worked there with me for a time, as an electrician. Even before going on the London mission, Cathal Brugha had asked me if I could recommend others, and I had suggested Joe. By then he must have been on the list of probables for our Active Service Unit. Certainly he was to go further than I then imagined. Bill Whelan, after failing to find employment in Dublin, finally returned to London.

On Armistice Day, the 11th of November, there was a good deal of pro-British demonstration in Dublin, and crowds walked the streets waving Union Jacks. It was hard to believe that but two years earlier, armed Irishmen had fought and died in those streets.

INSIDE THE GPO

I came across Paddy McGrath, who was quite seriously touring the town burning Union Jacks. First, he would squirt paraffin at the flag and then throw a weighted string, which was soaked in paraffin, over the pole – and set fire to the string, which acted like a fuse. Paddy did what he could and was cheerful about it.

I was angry, watching these demonstrators; I had been fired that day from my newest job at another firm, having left the shell factory. The foreman had found out by accident that I had a connection with the Volunteers. It was my first experience of this kind, and I could not take it with the resignation of the average Irishman, having experienced no such victimisation in England. That overly tolerant quality of the southern Irish in the face of injustice was beyond me; it was my temperament to hit back.

Amongst the Volunteers there were Protestants who, as always in Irish history, were among the best of the best. And these were within the inner core of the movement, as they had always been in the past. Liberal, highly educated and articulate Protestants were in the vanguard of the nationalist cause. But outside in the factories and workshops, there was a foreign element – though with Irish names – narrow, bigoted and spineless. I could almost recognise them by their appearance and mannerisms, but would have laughed if I had been told that in London. This element ruled the roost in many workshops, and the unionist expression, 'He digs with the right foot' or 'He digs with the wrong foot', I found to be revolting. Many Volunteers were fired from their jobs as far back as early 1916 for even being seen on parades. It still persisted. I could understand the massacre that preceded Cromwell's conquest. These were my thoughts as I watched the mafficking, the cheers which greeted the victory of British arms in Europe.

Counter-demonstrators appeared in the Dublin streets carrying tricolours, and scuffles took place all over the town. One group of young boys was carrying a tricolour, and was pursued by a number of British soldiers. They caught up with the boys at the very place where The O'Rahilly had fallen. I called to the boys to stand and thrash the soldiers, which – to my surprise – they did. They made such a thorough job of it that I felt a sense of self-disgust.

I left Moore Street and stood talking to a British private; he said how pitiful it was to see poor people, soldiers and civilians, behaving that way after a World War. I agreed, but did not tell him what I had just seen happen. The ambulances were busy, picking up people injured in the clashes between unionists and nationalists. It occurred to me, as it had on so many other occasions, that the British could not hold this country long if the people had arms in their hands. I had seen children thrash grown men.

IN THE COUNTRY, 1919–1920

From December of 1918 to April 1920, I was engaged in installing electric lighting plants in Wicklow, Mayo and Galway. Although I was still active in the Volunteer movement, with increasing skill as an electrician I was able to support myself more effectively, choosing to work mostly in the country areas. It was borne in on me repeatedly that small Irish towns and villages had one thing in common. Ruins.

Upon entering any town or village, one saw the stark remains of demolished cottages, the stones held together with what looked like mud. On leaving Drogheda, going north, one got the very strong impression that Cromwell had only recently passed through. I was struck by the nakedness of those villages and towns, where there were no small front gardens; no foliage anywhere.

I could not help comparing them with agricultural districts in Kent and Surrey, where the little old cottages were part of the landscape, as if they had grown out of the soil, an integral part of the surrounding country. The little English cottages I had lodged in sprang to my mind, where the people made simple wines and gave one a glass with pride. Their furnishings were treasured; how many years had it taken to make those deep feather beds and patchwork quilts? The whole interior glowed with a quiet contentment, like the village pub or inn where the labourers passed an evening. And the English labourer, a stocky man with straps below the knees, with a brass buckle on his belt and strong corduroy trousers, had no inferiority complex. He was a man who had his place in the scheme of things. His like was not to be found in Ireland. That expression I'd heard in Ireland, of 'only a labouring man', would be unintelligible to him. He drank his pint or so of light beer or cider, and sat an evening out while drinking it, and the innkeeper had to be civil to him or he would take his custom elsewhere.

And the English village policeman, working his front garden in his open tunic and straw hat, was unlike the Peeler or RIC policeman in Irish counties, with his rifle and suspicious stare.

Here in Ireland, the police stayed close to their quarters, and could not be seen in the context of home. Here, the stark streets overlooked by the police barracks were inhabited by a few dogs snapping at one's feet in the wide open road. It would be no sacrilege here to throw a hand-grenade. When nights were long and evenings short, there was nothing for the young men to do; their 'betters' had no interest in them. Their 'betters' were foreigners. Wealth in an English village implied social responsibility. Any form of activity in an Irish village was a godsend. One did not wonder why the people had fought and continued fighting. There was no obvious continuity in anything; even the Catholic church was very seldom one hundred years old. Perhaps it was the overlooking police barracks that was the cause of it all.

The RIC wore a dismal uniform of dark bottle-green. Whilst having the attributes of Cossacks, they lacked their picturesqueness. They were not without merit, however, for they bred numerous rebel sons. It must have been that uniform that produced the reaction. But they possessed what was the envy of thousands of Volunteers. Each had a splendid small carbine. The time was now long overdue when these should be taken away from them.

TRAINING OF VOLUNTEERS IN MAYO

During most of 1919, I was working in the west of Ireland, mainly in Mayo. 'The West', I found, was then anything but 'awake' – at least in some parts of that county. The west could only be awakened when arms were available: meanwhile, where were the arms?

Richard Walsh, later a TD in Dáil Éireann (a TD being the equivalent of an MP in the British parliament), was then living in Balla, County Mayo, and was a member of the executive of the Irish Volunteers. I co-operated with Dick, and assisted in the training of the Volunteers in his area. During this period, I met Peadar McMahon, who was later secretary in the Department of Defence in an Irish government. He was then organising officer of the Volunteers.

The organising officers in the Volunteers had the most wretched jobs. They were paid, I believe, about two pounds a week, barely enough to sustain them. They were constantly under observation and likely to be interrogated. Of necessity, they could not lodge with known sympathisers. They carried life insurance literature around with them as camouflage. Of all the jobs, organising was the most heartbreaking that an officer could be called upon to do, when there was no likelihood of action. And, in my opinion, it was rather too much to ask men in sparsely populated areas to travel great distances, merely to drill Volunteers without any weapons.

One incident stands out in my memory. A number of Volunteers were drilling, unarmed, in a stubble field. Present were an executive officer and an organising officer of the Volunteers. The owner of the field was protesting, although it was mid-winter and the men could do no harm by drilling. The farmer ordered all of us out of his field; whereupon the executive officer sarcastically offered him payment. The organising officer was angry and humiliated. It did not occur to either of them to threaten the farmer. We were gentle revolutionaries. I could sense the danger of the men's hearing this altercation, and believed we were on the point of giving way to the man, so I told him to get inside his house and shut his door or I would burn the roof over his head. He fled, and the Volunteers were able to resume their drill. The joke was that I had no particular authority – at least in that matter – and one of those two officers was to become Chief of Staff of the new Irish army, and the other was one of the most determined men I have known. They both risked their lives willingly for years, and yet simply could not suddenly do violence to anyone's feelings – not even those of an enemy – when the occasion demanded it.

It seemed once that there was a chance of some action, when Jack Plunkett arrived in Balla, County Mayo. By one of those ludicrous accidents that were always happening, he stopped his car outside Dick Walsh's house, Dick being then a member of the executive of the Volunteers. Plunkett immediately made an enquiry about Dick's whereabouts, which, of course, made those he spoke to suspicious. Someone came to me and told me that a man was looking for Walsh, 'who says he's Jack Plunkett. Would you know him?'

I walked past the car, whistling a few bars from 'The Heather Glen', and this was answered immediately by the following bar. So I knew then that this was from someone familiar with our old Kimmage password, as it was a method we had used at the Kimmage garrison on the Plunkett estate early in 1916.

Jack Plunkett stepped out of the car, and I told him he could be observed from the police barracks, and to take the car to a less conspicuous place. Lord French was staying in a nearby part of Mayo during this period, but no attempt had been made either to attack or kidnap him, and I thought Jack might have brought orders to set this in motion. Jack had come to Mayo that time on less significant business. Some weeks later, however, Lord French was tackled. I had heard the news of that attack, and of the death of Martin Savage,[51] an old comrade of mine, on a day that was to end with a Volunteer dance – a big community *céilí* to which the whole town was invited. Martin Savage had been a member of my own company in Dublin in the Volunteers, and I was very fond of him.

That turned out to be a very strange Volunteer *céilí* dance. There was a British soldier in uniform dancing in the hall. Because I was angry and sad at the death of a comrade, I approached the MC and protested at their allowing a soldier in British uniform to be present on such an occasion. He gave me no answer, but I learned that the soldier in British uniform was related to our own local district inspector. I had been out all day drilling, and had then done what I had never done before or since – drunk the greater part of a bottle of port. Possibly as a result of this, I made a scene and ordered the soldier out of the hall – and then proceeded to address the assembled dancers. What I said I do not know, but it must have impressed the dancers: the *céilí* broke up in disorder.

The following day, I was utterly ashamed of myself, and reluctant to face the people of the town; I was particularly

---

51 Savage was killed in the Ashtown ambush, 19 December 1919, an attempt to assassinate the Viceroy, Lord French.

afraid of two ladies with whom I lodged, who'd been present at the dance, though they did not know that I had taken any drink. Perhaps I had carried the drink well. But I ran when I saw them. One of them ran after me, and put her arms around my neck, saying, 'You did right, Joe!'; and her companion said also, 'Oh, but you did right, surely!' This was very surprising to me, for they were both frivolous youngsters.[52]

The next Sunday, I went back to the hall – intending perhaps to give the soldier some satisfaction – but this didn't prove to be necessary. It transpired that he did not return to the British army, but joined the Volunteers and became a good officer. There's something to be said for port wine. I'm glad the town didn't know the alcoholic cause of the scene, although I saw from this incident how easy it was to awaken them to a sense of their duty.

During my stay in Mayo, an oath of allegiance to Dáil Éireann was administered to all Volunteers. Michael Staines came to Balla, and the meeting of officers of the Mayo Brigade was held in a shed in the convent grounds. This meeting was addressed by Michael Staines, and there were about one hundred men present, who, I was told, were Volunteer officers. Although I thought that the oath of allegiance to the Dáil was necessary, I considered it rather amusing, since most of those

---

52 Joe, being merely twenty-four at this time, was himself little more than a youngster, though hardly a frivolous one.

men, to my knowledge, were members of the Irish Republican Brotherhood – who must already have taken such an oath.

I have one reason to remember Christmas of 1919 very clearly. I'd returned for a few days to the house I rented at 109 Richmond Road in Drumcondra. George Plunkett was staying for a few days with me – he was then on the run. I had come home late, and did not notice another guest as well as George in the spare bedroom. When I awoke, I heard someone talking to George in an emphatic, cultivated English accent, and then discovered that it was Desmond Fitzgerald. Desmond had been our quartermaster in the GPO during the Rising, and I had often wanted to tell him what I thought of him and his rations; he had given me a bun and a cup of tea after four days of eating only chocolate. I called out from my bed, 'Is that Desmond Fitzgerald! My God – I've waited for three years in hopes of telling you what I thought of you and your starvation measures, and now you are my guest: there's no justice in the world!' Yet I also remembered then, and still do, how much Fitzgerald had endured and achieved on behalf of our movement, long before 1916. Still, it was pleasant to have a chance to tick him off.

1920

I WAS ORDERED back to Dublin early in 1920. Dublin city itself was comparatively quiet during the early part of the year, despite – or even because of – our successful action against the British secret service, especially when a number of their best intelligence officers were shot. Collins was on the attack. And despite some political objections, I heard no comment from Dubliners themselves, adverse or otherwise, on those shootings.

In the south of Ireland, particularly in Limerick, there had been sensational attacks on barracks. This seemed surprising to Volunteers in Dublin – at least it was to me – and I was anxious to know from whence this fervour sprang. So I wrote to Garret MacAuliffe, who was then brigadier of west Limerick, I think, and he asked me to come down to Limerick, and to bring some stuff with me.

It was arranged that I take down to Limerick hand-grenades, revolvers and ammunition. It looked to me as if our GHQ was particularly generous with arms and ammunition where there was real military action. I took to Limerick nearly one hundredweight of varied ammunition – some hand-grenades the size of Mills bombs, and some as large as coconuts.

Garret MacAuliffe had told me to 'make no arrangements' and that I would be 'picked up'. The terms were vague, but knowing Garret well, I was satisfied that he would make an 'arrangement' that would work. On my journey to Limerick, I actually conversed with a young Englishman who was en route to join the RIC in Cork.

I changed trains at Limerick Junction. About sixty RIC men were waiting to board the same local train as myself. I went to the extreme other end of the train, and found a dirty carriage in which were a large number of plate-layers and railway workers. These men must have sensed my predicament, for, when I hurriedly entered their carriage, they all crowded at the windows and deterred the RIC from entering our portion of the already-crowded train.

I expected to be met at Rathkeale Station, but this was not the case. On alighting, I found myself alone. I was carrying a clerical hatbox that was big enough to contain a bishop's mitre – but which was packed tight with ammunition and grenades.

A number of the local RIC had met the train, apparently to guard the larger number of RIC who were travelling further south. As both of my hands were engaged with my packages, and as I would have to pass the RIC in order to leave the station, I departed by a little side entrance. A porter promptly saw my difficulty, took the ticket from where I held it between my teeth and opened the little gate quickly for me. Outside the station was a small pony-and-trap. 'Ah,' thought I, 'this is the "arrangement" for me to be picked up.' I put my ammunition into the trap and climbed into it myself, but a little girl who was sitting in the trap was about to scream. I alighted from the trap with my packages, and said that I had made a mistake; that I thought the trap belonged to somebody else.

The station for Rathkeale is some distance from the town proper. I was walking very slowly towards the town when the local RIC group eventually caught up with me. I asked them to assist me in carrying my packages, and this they did very civilly. Perhaps my clergyman's innocuous hatbox saved the situation. It occurred to me at that moment that it was the only logical tactic to disarm suspicion.

Some 300 yards or so outside Rathkeale, I entered a poor dwelling, a one-room cottage. I asked the woman of the house if it was possible to leave my larger parcel there. She said, 'Well, certainly, young fellow,' although she had no idea of its nature or contents. Then I asked if I might put the parcel under the bed – by which time she must have suspected something. Yet she still said, 'Most certainly,' and pushed it gently under the bed. There was dire poverty in that cottage.

With only one small suitcase, I went to a nearby hotel, ordered lunch and went to the commercial room. I noticed at once that the commercial room was in considerable disorder. Plaster from the ceiling was thick on the floor and tables, the mirrors and windows were smashed – obviously by gunfire. For a long time I waited for lunch. Meanwhile, I took a revolver from my suitcase and loaded it. It was very quiet. Far too quiet.

Suddenly the doors burst open and Garret MacAuliffe came into the room. He was openly armed: there was a gun in the holster that was hanging at his side, and he was wearing a Sam Browne belt accoutred with bulging cartridge pouches. Apart from his very dusty Volunteer officer's uniform, he might have been something out of the American Wild West.

This sudden apparition was a bit of a shock to me, and I said, 'Is there a war on here?'

'Get out at once, Joe. I've a car at the door. I know where you left the ammunition. It'll come on later.'

I got into a Ford car with him as he said, 'Have you a gun?'

'Yes.'

'Is it loaded?'

'Yes. What's up?'

'We tried to hold up your train and ran into a party of military.'

This incident of my meeting with an old mate was typical of the prevailing atmosphere in Limerick, or at least in that part of the county where Garret MacAuliffe was operating. It soon became clear to me that open war was in full progress. All the Volunteers that I was to see there carried arms openly, and they seemed in very real possession of many towns and villages. Many of the RIC barracks had fallen, and I could feel that it wouldn't be too long before Garret and his men would make their move on the city of Limerick itself.[53]

Garret explained to me – among many other astonishing things over the next few days – that the hotel in which I had endeavoured to get lunch had been the scene of an action about a week before my visit, in which MacAuliffe and other Volunteers had executed the district inspector of the RIC and some British intelligence officers. Yet very curious situations still existed, or were allowed to exist if they served the eccentric functioning of the MacAuliffe brigade. For instance, in this town of Rathkeale, it was very common for the Volunteers to enter the town at dusk – following a day of very active campaigning – and to be challenged by the British army sentry, whilst they actually put the carbines

---

53 As a boy in the late 'forties, I returned home from a cycling trip once to find Garret MacAuliffe visiting my father. Recounting my trip, I remarked that I found Limerick a surprisingly attractive city, and asked Garret if he knew it. 'Know it?' he replied. 'I took it!'

with which they were armed behind their backs, answered the challenge, and entered the houses where they sometimes passed the night.

Here, in this part of County Limerick at least, that Republic that Garret and myself had heard proclaimed in Easter Week was, in many fundamental ways, in established existence. The regular British army was, to an amazing extent, stalemated and non-combatant – leaving, as it were, a clear field of fire between the Volunteers and the local police or RIC forces.

It was this incapacity of the regular British troops to cope with the new guerrilla tactics of the Volunteers, developed by Mick Collins and his commanders of 'Flying Columns', which would soon lead to the English enlistment of irregulars and 'Black and Tan' auxiliaries against us, in the final phase of the War of Independence, for which Collins had so long planned. And which men like Garret were now bringing to fruition.

The Volunteers in these areas were extremely popular and were made much of, especially by the matrons of the households. As ever, in the new tradition of the Volunteers of the Rising and what was now emerging throughout the whole country, these young men were sober, usually pious and, like many Irish countrymen, well-mannered and courteous. In the houses of this district, it was quite common to hear from the people of those households, 'Easy now, be quiet now – we have so many of the boys here.' The speaker would then mention the number of 'the boys' in the house.

It was also very common to hear these same householders claim, 'We have – so many – "Bottles" here,' again mentioning the number: 'perhaps a dozen, or more!' The 'bottles' were prototypes of the Russian partisan 'Molotov Cocktails', filled with paraffin oil for use in raids on police barracks. Those bottles and other lethal things were collected zealously.

It struck me that hatred of the enemy went very deep. The following incident illustrates what I mean.

During our attack on Kilmallock Barracks, one of the Volunteer attackers was heard to shout out, 'Come out, Bruce, and surrender – this isn't '67!'

When I inquired into this incident, I discovered that the RIC man being called out was a grandnephew of one of the men who had occupied that same barracks in 1867, and the Volunteer was a grandnephew of one of the earlier attackers.

I was told that the local senior Catholic clergyman in the town of Rathkeale was very hostile to the Volunteers. We were all very chary about taking full advantage of his church grounds, though they were excellent routes of advance or retreat. Perhaps his attitude to us was not so surprising, when one considered what had now become of his flock.

Sean Finn, or Jackie Finn as we called him, was the officer-in-charge of the Mid-Limerick Brigade. Rathkeale was his area. For the most part, active Volunteer groups were limited to eight or ten men. Ease of mobility was one reason for this limit.[54]

The lack of effective arms was a much more important reason. These men travelled around sometimes in two Ford cars, and were frequently compelled to carry out duties that should normally have been performed by our area commandants. On one occasion, an area commandant was unwilling, or too gentle, to carry out the execution of a spy, and a member of the brigade staff was forced to perform this duty ...

During one of our halts for rest one day, while out on our 'flying column' routes, Sean Moylan and Liam Lynch came to join us in a Daimler car. It was a very cumbersome affair, and I wondered how long it must have taken them to come from Cork. They were very nonchalant, and obviously inured to living dangerously. It pained me to see the condition of the engine – though I'm no real mechanic – and the defectiveness of the brakes must have been more dangerous than any challenge from the enemy. It was impossible, as I watched them take off swaying down the muddy road, not to think back to the loss of those other valuable men when that car went into the sea in Kerry in Easter Week.

---

54 Sean Finn's small force being an excellent and typical example of the 'flying columns'.

CAPTURE OF GENERAL LUCAS

The day following their visit, I think, some eight of us, with Jackie Finn in charge, went to Cork to take over a prisoner, General Lucas, whom that most Active Service Unit had captured.

Sean Moylan and Liam Lynch had captured him at Kanturk. It took a considerable time for our small group to get to Mitchelstown, where they had him in custody. The whole party of us, including Sean Moylan and Liam Lynch, came back from Cork to Templeglantine, where our prisoner was to be lodged that night.

Lucas was the traditional British officer. He appeared to be quite a simple man, apart from the military veneer that his training had given him. During our first conversation, Lucas was looking down over the valley from that hill at Templeglantine. It was a very beautiful view, and from where we stood we could see a number of counties. He remarked to me, 'This is a country worth fighting for.'

'That's a peculiar comment,' I said. 'It reminds me that another general – your predecessor, Cromwell – once made a similar remark.'

Lucas smiled slowly and he said, 'Yes, I believe I remember reading something about that somewhere.'

Then, curious I suppose about my accent, which was still then much more London than Irish, he asked, 'But what, if you'll pardon my asking, has you so far from home?'

I explained that my mother's people had been exiled from County Cork, just to the south of us, and my father's family had originally had their homes in County Tipperary – just to the east – before being driven out in the famine years. Lucas remained quietly thinking for some time, before smiling more broadly and saying, 'Well, that's a long way back, it would appear, to Tipperary.'

We continued to talk, casually but with increasing familiarity, as the sun set over that landscape of the Golden Vale of County Limerick. I pointed out that we were within spitting distance of the lands confiscated by Elizabeth and handed to Spenser, and where he had retired to write his Faerie Queene. Lucas quoted some stanza from Spenser's poem, and then stopped abruptly – and added after a long pause, 'I suppose it's high time that the natives resumed care of the Four Green Fields.'

This, I remember, surprised me even more: an English officer being familiar with that idea of the 'Four Green Fields', the old image in Irish poetry for the four provinces of Ireland, those four 'fields' of 'Cathleen Ni Houlihan'.

'Yes,' I said. 'You are right – these are all worth fighting for.'

It struck me then that General Lucas was connected with some of the ruling families of England. I started to abuse the ruling classes of England, and concentrated on the Cecils. He defended them. Soon after, we said good night and went to our separate quarters.

Two days later, some of us escorted Lucas to the banks of the Shannon. Michael Brennan arrived in a punt or boat. It was late in the night, and there was no attempt to blindfold Lucas, which I thought somewhat foolish. The general was calmly and concentratedly observing the stars. He was to prove to us all later that he was an excellent soldier, and a resourceful navigator. Mick Brennan took Lucas across the Shannon, and I remained in County Limerick. I was wondering if I would ever have the pleasure of the general's company again. I hoped so. He was a generous-hearted man.

IN ACTION WITH SEAN FINN

A few days after Lucas had departed, our party – the staff of the Mid-Limerick Brigade – were resting in the priest's house in Ballyhahill. I had always thought that those countrymen were rather careless, since they rarely mounted guards in the daytime. On this occasion, we were playing cards when someone warned us that the RIC enemy had entered the village. It was quite a small party, perhaps no more than five or six, and it transpired that they were not seeking us; they were simply in the public house, getting some refreshments. I suggested to Jackie Finn that as I would not arouse suspicion, on account of the way I dressed and the way I spoke, I could enter the public house and call upon them to surrender. This would have been easy to do, because we had plenty of hand-grenades, but Jackie said he could not agree to this, as the whole village would be wiped out later. I would not have suggested this action had I not felt assured that I, personally, would be safe.

Eventually the RIC party left the village and proceeded to Glin, which was about three miles distant. Jackie Finn said he had decided to attack them on their return journey – some distance away from our village of Ballyhahill. During the ambush that subsequently took place between Glin and Ballyhahill, I saw the pathetic weakness of our Volunteers – a weakness in military tactics and in basic instinct for sound manoeuvre.

We had taken up our positions in a ditch. On the far side of the roadway, the river flowed. We had approached our position from a very oblique direction – and up a slight incline. Consequently, I was not aware that the ground behind us was exceedingly steep. I assumed that these Limerick Volunteers had their own proven tactics and strategy, but I noticed that most of our men were very close together (too close for my taste), so I went some distance away from them, in the direction from which the enemy would approach.

The enemy party came along on bicycles. From our position in the ditch, we could not fully see their approach, nor had we a good field of fire. Only two of the enemy were allowed to ride into the ambush, or two that I could see.

These were fired on and fell. There was further firing for a bit – and then silence. I was on the extreme flank and expected an order, but there was no order. Then, suddenly, one of the enemy attempted to cross the ditch immediately beside me. There was time only to turn on my back and fire at him. I presumed I had hit him, but from my position it was difficult to be certain.

I tried to reload my carbine, and found that I could not eject the spent cartridge case. Suddenly I heard Jackie Finn say loudly, 'Where is Joe?' His call attracted my attention, and I saw that my comrades were on the move. When I turned my head, I could see our attacking party creeping away up the steep hill behind us. There must have been a number of survivors among the enemy, as there was firing from three or four of their rifles.

Then we were running up the steep hill. I called out, 'Return their fire.'

One of our lads immediately lay down and began to do so. I flopped down beside him, took my bolt out of my jammed carbine, and was thus able to get the cartridge case out and reload.

Our return fire was sporadic, and not as effective as I hoped; but I want to make it clear that these Volunteers were armed with carbines, which were good enough weapons, but their ammunition did not always fit. There was then a Mark VI and a Mark VII issue of ammunition for those weapons by the British government, and we very obviously had the wrong cartridges.

This abortive ambush made several things clear to me: that the Volunteers in that area had received no instruction or training for guerrilla warfare; that there was no regard for lines of retreat; and that our men did not realise that they could be enfiladed, as they were.

Our party were six or seven in number, but with only four of those RIC carbines between us. I think our commander, Sean Finn, had a service rifle or revolver. But even those few carbines we had were on loan from the East-Limerick Brigade. And this was in July 1920. Although our party had probably practised both loading and unloading, they had not, until then, actually fired the carbines, because of the scarcity of ammunition. And any gun, of course, must be fired in training to ascertain how it will later behave in action. In view of our ludicrously small resources, it was a miracle that so many of the actions fought were as successful as they were.

Sean Finn, our brigadier, was twenty-two years of age. He was a most conscientious Volunteer officer, and maintained good discipline and care of his men. Also, it was quite clear that several of the enemy were firing as we retreated, so it was obvious that their numbers had been increased in the town of Glin. Jackie Finn acted wisely and correctly in vacating our position under those circumstances.

The fault of a jammed cartridge was later the cause of another failure, in another part of Limerick. And I made these facts very clear to Mick Collins when I was later asked to make my report to our GHQ in Dublin.

Still, it was a long, difficult progress we made, up into the hills that evening, and it was some time before our rear-guard was able to withdraw and join up with the rest of our column. The enemy abandoned their pursuit, which would have been pointless in any case as we melted into the country lanes. That evening, we were sheltered in a very modest cottage, where we were served with hot tea and stew. One of the daughters of the house baked us a fresh cake of soda bread. It was the best soda bread I've ever tasted.

FURTHER CONVERSATIONS WITH GENERAL LUCAS

Shortly after that ambush near Glin, I received a dispatch from Michael Brennan, asking me to come to County Clare. Some suspicious visitors had been installed in a hotel, near to the place where General Lucas was held prisoner. Lucas and his guard – and this included Mick Brennan – were quartered in a big house near Meelick, in County Clare.

While I was in Limerick, I had intercepted a telegram that was addressed to Lucas. This was addressed to 'General Lucas, C/O The Shin Feiners, Irish Republican Army, Cork.' We were getting known ...

This missive was an encouraging, if not flattering, indication that the enemy 'authorities' were apparently coming to terms with our existence, though they were as confused as ever regarding our varied nomenclature.

That telegram ran something like this: 'BORN THIS MORNING A SON. BOTH DOING WELL,' and then the wife's name. The telegram had been sent to Cork city, was abstracted and a copy brought to us in Limerick by our dispatch rider. It's worth noting that our communications, on both local and national levels, were by then very probably superior to those of the British.

After modifying the date of arrival, I took this telegram with me to County Clare. Brennan gave the telegram to Lucas, who expressed surprise and thanks. It referred to his first-born child. Lucas noticed the time stamped on the telegram: it had – seemingly – taken only a few hours to reach him. He complimented me on this later. It did not occur to him that the time and the date might have been an artistic touch. I rather prided myself on that.

The place in which Lucas was then held prisoner had, I thought, a fantastic air. Four rifles were piled in the centre of the drawing room, which had an elegant Turkish carpet. We dined at eight. We played tennis, often, in the afternoons. Sometimes I had to request Lucas to cease playing and withdraw to a clump of trees, as we could be seen from passing military lorries, and he might very easily have been recognised.

Lucas and I did some fishing on the Shannon, a great river for salmon or trout, but he caught nothing. However, on one occasion he caught me – saving me from a ducking or worse. I was being swept towards the weir at Castleconnel when I was alone in a punt. Mick Brennan thought I was joking when I shouted that I could not control my punt, but Lucas jumped into another boat and managed to tow me ashore. Mick Brennan and the other Volunteers on the riverbank then informed me that they could not swim. General Lucas certainly could, however, and he might have availed of this opportunity to escape.

Lucas was very frank. He told me that if he was released or exchanged for one of our men in British custody, he had decided that he would not again take service in Ireland. He appeared to be embarrassed by the intimate knowledge he had of us personally, and of the houses and places where he had been kept prisoner. He once said to me, 'In the event of my release, I shall be asked questions. I know you all, person-ally, and know that you carry arms.'

I replied, 'That is our right, and we ask no defence of it.'

There was another of those little pauses. He smiled and said 'Anyhow ... It is unlikely that any of you fellows will be caught alive.'

I thought that was very nice of him, but I reported our conversation to Mick Brennan at once. Mick saw what Lucas was driving at, and told me to follow up that conversation.

Later, I said to Lucas, 'Many of the houses and people to which we have taken you have sheltered you and us out of their innate hospitality. They would have treated British soldiers of your rank-and-file similarly. We are all conscious of this, and hope that they will not suffer as a result of their kindness.'

Lucas replied to this immediately, by saying, 'I shall not say where I have been lodged.'

And in this he kept his word.

During our conversations together, which were becoming more frequent, as he apparently felt very much at ease with me – perhaps because of the typical confidence of his class – Lucas seemed to be sounding me out as a possible channel in connection with our GHQ. His instinct in this was justified, perhaps, as I invariably reported anything that I gleaned from him to my superiors.

Lucas told me that he was convinced that a 'new party' was about to be formed in England, and that Lord Hugh and Robert Cecil would probably form part of that government; that some sort of 'Dominion Home Rule' would form part of their programme; that, in any case, there was to be a Labour Party government in England, soon; and that we would be 'foolish to be forcing the pace at this time'.

Of course, Irishmen everywhere, including those born in England like myself, have been given this story throughout the ages. There was a sense in which Lucas, even perhaps thinking of me as an intermediary – albeit a minor one – could not help believing that he was informing a country boy, and that his remarks were intended to combat my prejudices. Of course, I was anything but a country boy, but Mick Collins (who savoured this chat when it was reported to him) was both a country boy and something more – the new man in Irish affairs, who could deal effectively with the old politics of a General Lucas.

Lucas said one thing to me that was startling: 'You have the pick of the country. I could match you if I had the pick of England.'

That remark foretold the Auxiliaries and the 'Black and Tans'[55] who would be soon launched against us from England. Though that 'pick' of Britain was to lack one essential – and that was our moral discipline.

Some time later, General Lucas asked for parole, saying that he would return to any place we would like to name. He said that he wanted to see his wife and child. I considered this development to be a major coup for us, and we dispatched this information to our GHQ immediately. But our adjutant-general, Gearoid O'Sullivan, replied that even if Lucas were incommoded, he would have to remain a prisoner.

55 Police reinforcements, which began arriving in March and August 1920 respectively, and were noted for their indiscriminate brutality. The Black and Tans were so called from the colour of their uniforms, after the hounds of a famous hunt. The Auxiliaries (the Police Auxiliary Cadets) wore blue uniforms and Glengarry caps.

We thought this decision rather stupid. Considerable prestige would have been gained by us if we had availed, right then, of this offer of parole. Our GHQ could have then made it totally conditional on the release of Terence MacSwiney, Lord Mayor of Cork city, who was then in jail and in danger of dying on his already lengthy hunger strike.[56] But it apparently did not occur to our adjutant-general that a high-ranking British officer could make such a proposal, and might have exercised pressure on the British politicians. A great opportunity, I thought then – and still think – had been lost.

It was quite easy for General Lucas to know where he was lodged. We stayed in Bunratty Castle, Clare Castle and some other large dwelling-houses of the gentry, where there was writing material bearing the address of the house. In one old house, there was a rowing scull bearing the name of a famous old Oxford 'Blue'.

Meanwhile, poor Mick Brennan was anxious to be rid of the continuing responsibility for Lucas, and often said to me that the Clare Volunteers were forced to be inactive whilst guarding him. His most frequent complaint was something like, 'Ah dammit, Joe, we're going stale on this nanny's work!'

But the orders would keep coming to move on and find another hiding place. In one humble home where Lucas was lodged, he slept between sheets made of flour bags. We had given him some whiskey before retiring one night, as he

---

56 Terence MacSwiney died very soon after.

was wet. In the morning, he told us he thought he'd had a nightmare, for his sheets appeared to be covered with black men's heads. He was right. These were the imprinted heads of black African labourers on those crude white flour-bags from which the sheets had been stitched.

I finally left the Clare Brigade to go back to Dublin. Mick Brennan gave me some dispatches, and told me to inform GHQ of the latest that I had gleaned from my conversations with General Lucas. I said goodbye to the general, and never saw him again. He was a kindly man: he had once offered to put a stitch on a small wound that I had collected.

A LUCKY ESCAPE

When I left Clare, I delivered a dispatch in Limerick and then cycled to Limerick Junction. As I cycled through the village of Oola, a military cordon was flung across the road behind me. My front tyre was punctured. I entered a public house to get some refreshment and make inquiries, but as I entered, I tripped on a step and fell into the laps of three RIC men. I tried to disarm their suspicions, but when I had finished my drink, they followed me out. I cycled on toward Limerick Junction on a flat tyre. The three RIC men were still behind me, so I took to a footpath that led more directly to my objective of the railway station. As I was cycling fast – on a now flayed tyre – anyone coming my way had to jump clear. The train was at the junction; it had started to move, but I had faith and still pedalled hard. Then, one of those very unexpected things happened.

The driver stopped the train, the guard came to the crossing, took my bicycle and put it on the train, and I jumped aboard, and the police – who were still following me – were left standing at the railway crossing. They had very nearly caught me. It was a very pleasant moment, to stand on that train and watch the image of those RIC men receding into the far distance.

DUBLIN AGAIN

I reached Dublin that evening, and went to report to our GHQ; but I found that no one was there. So I then felt free to go to a *céilí* – a Volunteer dance advertised to be taking place in the Mansion House. The *céilí* was being held at the conclusion of the festival of the Oireachtas.[57]

Getting back to my home at 109 Richmond Road was a little tricky, as the British curfew was in force until 3:30am at that time. Dublin seemed strangely peaceful after the various excitements that I had experienced down in the country.

---

57 The Oireachtas was a formal gathering, celebration and dance, including competitions in Gaelic dance and music – a social and community occasion that was, effectively, a major cultural event for a then almost fully autonomous Irish national government. It is still held annually.

I saw most of our GHQ staff at that céilí: Mick Collins and Gearoid O'Sullivan, Dick Mulcahy and others. Our GHQ may have attended this function for the sake of morale, and regarded it as being perfectly safe because so many of the enemy secret service had by now been wiped out.

There was at last a feeling in our movement that we could be winning. There was an adaptation of a popular song that was sung by the Volunteers during this period. It was to the air of 'Pop-goes-the-Weazel!' but the final line, as the Volunteers sang it, was 'Pop-goes-the-Peeler!' This little song expressed a phase when our movement had the initiative, when the Volunteers were learning to be ruthless, and which was an historic development from the romanticism of 1916.

I told Mick Collins at that *céilí* that I had just come from the south, and that I had dispatches, and he told me to see our adjutant general, Gearoid O'Sullivan, who ordered me to report to Suffolk Street on the following day. I recall that Mick looked very tired, but – and there is no other word for it – triumphant. I know that I handed over my dispatches the following day at our headquarters, but cannot remember whether I saw Gearoid O'Sullivan or not.

POSTSCRIPT FROM GENERAL LUCAS

There was to be a remarkable sort of coda to the General Lucas business. Having been refused his parole, Lucas must have decided, quite possibly for entirely personal reasons, to make an absurdly daring escape from the custody of the Volunteers.[58] Knowing the man's character as I did, it was no surprise to me that he fought his way to freedom with such spectacular success.

I decided to go to London on a mission to gather arms at that time, because I did not wish, then, to be questioned by our GHQ. I was still feeling too furious at our lost opportunity in failing to trade General Lucas for Terence MacSwiney – and also because of the recent resultant and needless death of MacSwiney. I was also reflecting that Liam Lynch, who had captured Lucas with the very specific aim of protecting MacSwiney, would be very justifiably angry.

After spending nine or ten days in London, I returned to Dublin, and en route conversed with two British soldiers who were also travelling on my train to Holyhead. They were both returning from a short leave for their next tour-of-duty in Ireland.

On this – as on many other occasions – my London accent made it easy for me to communicate with British soldiers. There has always been a naive assumption that an English accent precludes any Irish republican allegiance.

Neither soldier was exactly relishing the thought of what lay ahead. One of those soldiers showed very considerable

---

58 Tim Pat Coogan, in Michael Collins (1990), maintains that Michael Brennan, fed up with his 'nannying', engineered Lucas' escape.

fear; there was almost a sense of awe in his regard for the 'Sin-Fanyers', as he called us.

This soldier told me a remarkable story.

He said that he was a batman to some English general, whose name I cannot now remember. He told me that before going on his just-completed leave, he had been brought from his billet (I cannot remember the name of the barracks now) to the barracks gate, where a man was clamouring for admission.

This man was General Lucas, and he was in rags. Lucas had been ambushed – after he had evidently managed to escape from the Volunteers. Lucas told them that he had escaped by leaving his room in his stocking feet. He said that he had been picked up on the road by a post office van, which was being escorted by three or more soldiers; that the van had been attacked by Volunteer forces; that General Lucas had got a small wound across the bridge of his nose during the lengthy firing; that one of the soldiers was shot through the head, and his brains were inside his 'tin 'at' (steel helmet); that the escort was on the point of surrender when General Lucas picked up the dead man's rifle and opened fire on the IRA attackers; that the attackers withdrew, and that Lucas then came on to the barracks – where this soldier met him.

The soldier told me that Lucas then packed up the clothes which he had been wearing – sports coat and trousers – and told him to post these to an address in Cork city.

INSIDE THE GPO

During the detention of Lucas by the Volunteers, there was some definite house in Cork city to which communications were addressed, and from which they were sometimes subsequently delivered to him. It was to this address that he had the parcel dispatched, containing some garments with which we had provided him. Inside this package he left a note addressed, 'To the Sinn Féiners, or to the IRA, with the compliments of General Lucas.'

CONTACTS IN LONDON FOR THE SUPPLY OF ARMS

During my earlier short trip to London, I had met two men endeavouring to procure arms for export to the Volunteers, but I do not know if they had what could be termed a regular system of dispatch. One of these men was Edmond Browne; the other his brother, Bob Browne, who was soon to be married to my sister, Agnes. Bob Browne had not long before returned home, after some years in Canada and the United States; he had a slight American accent, and perpetually smoked a pipe or rolled cigarettes from a pouch of Bull Durham, and was then living in Islington in London. When I met the man that Bob was in contact with, a South African or an Australian (I'm not sure which), I learned that he had at his disposal some of the British surplus war equipment. I had no means of buying stuff in such bulk, or of transporting it to Ireland. And though I assumed that Robert Browne was in contact with our GHQ, I'd little faith, even at this late date, that he could buy that material, because he told me that he had already bought as many guns and ammunition as he could afford out of his own pocket. He was a working man.

Shortly after returning to Dublin, I had a meeting with Sean Finn, and told him of the ammunition and equipment that might be obtained in London. Sean asked me to make every effort to acquire some of that material. He said that the Limerick people had subscribed £2,000, which had been given to the Volunteers. I understood from what Finn said that the Irish authorities, which had by then taken the place of the disintegrating British administration, had levied the rates to acquire this sum of money, which was then in Sean Finn's possession.

While I'd been operating with the Limerick Volunteers, I frequently had very large sums of paper money in my hip pocket, as had all the others, but we had no opportunity or desire to spend that money, because it was usual for the people of Limerick to provide us with all that we needed. Sean Finn paid his party one pound per week to every man.

Sean offered me any quantity of this money that I wanted, and asked me to try and do something to improve the military equipment of the Limerick Brigade. I took sixty pounds – a large sum of money in those days – and returned to London a week or so later. When I reached Islington, I was informed by Bob Browne that, for some reason, the man who was selling the surplus ammunition had become nervous, and had disposed of it elsewhere.

Fortunately, before leaving for Dublin on my earlier trip, I had told a Cork Volunteer that this man – the South African – had two machine-guns. And the Corkman – as was very characteristic of Corkmen – had got on the job at once and secured one of the machine-guns, which, I believe, he had exported from Liverpool. I had very little success in procuring arms myself – I may have got two or three revolvers.

I returned to Dublin. I had spent a good deal of the money that I had taken with me, and I was somewhat ashamed that I had produced so little. I wrote to Garret MacAuliffe and told him that, so far, I had done little. So I went back to work in Dublin, with a view to supplementing what I had left – about thirty pounds – proposing to return to London when I had saved enough money to bring my funds at least up to the original amount given me by Sean Finn. During this period in Dublin, I worked with the firm of Thomas Dockrell and Sons, but my mind was constantly filled with the urgent need for arms.

PLAN TO PENETRATE HEADQUARTERS OF THE AUXILIARIES

In late 1920, the reign of terror unleashed by the Black and Tans and British Auxiliaries was reaching its peak, and

Collins had no choice – to protect our own GHQ – but to order the complete elimination of no less than fourteen of their 'intelligence' men in a single, co-ordinated operation. This was carried out by members of our ASU 'Squad', who suffered a few casualties. On that same day, 21 November ('Bloody Sunday'), the Auxiliaries retaliated by arriving in lorries during a Gaelic football game in Croke Park and opening fire on the civilian crowd, killing fourteen and wounding another fifty or sixty people.

Less than a week after 'Bloody Sunday', I went into the Auxiliaries' headquarters in Beggar's Bush Barracks, Dublin, relying as usual on my London accent and manner.

I knocked on the door and asked to see the engineer-in-charge, assuming there would be an engineer. I was taken to a Sergeant Major Dominie. I proposed to him that he install an independent lighting plant in Beggar's Bush and in other barracks throughout Ireland, as the enemy might soon resort to cutting a city power supply. My object was to recruit from our own Volunteers for such work – with a view to our then penetrating the organisation of the Auxiliaries.

Sergeant Major Dominie was much taken by my suggestion. I had told him that the 'Shinners' were certainly capable of plunging the entire city of Dublin into darkness. He asked me to come and see him again early – about eight o'clock – on the following day.

INSIDE THE GPO

So I arrived at Beggar's Bush Barracks at eight o'clock next morning. It was a foggy day. Two British guards preceded me to the inner gates. They were Black and Tans in mufti. I was admitted to a guardroom. While waiting in the guardroom, I realised that many of the Black and Tans were on the point of hysteria, for they were all constantly fiddling with their guns.

After too long a wait for my comfort, I demanded to see Sergeant Major Dominie, and was at length escorted to what was afterwards to become the orderly room of our national army. My interview with Sergeant-Major Dominie took place on the top floor of the building. I submitted an engineering plan, with an estimate of quantities of material needed – dynamos, engines, etc. Dominie told me he would communicate with me later. For references, I told him he could ring up Thomas Dockrell[59] immediately, whom I asserted I knew personally – which was stretching the truth a little.

On coming down the stairs after leaving the Sergeant Major, I was preceded by my Auxiliary escort, and I took a chance and opened a door on the right-hand side. This would have been the orderly room. I immediately saw a high-ranking officer, who I assumed was Major General Crozier – for he looked like him – sitting at a table. There were several women typists in the room. My rather sudden

---

59 Head of the firm where Joe was working.

appearance in civilian dress caused what I can only describe as a small panic in that room. One of the Tans angrily pulled me from the open door, and after we left the building he said to me, 'You got into this ... place – now you can bloody well get out!'

I crossed the square towards the gate alone. I passed an armed guard escorting a prisoner. It was Seamus McNamara, who had been arrested for the Mount Street shootings,[60] and he saw me. We both pretended not to recognise each other.

Getting out of the barracks could have presented real problems, but I succeeded by something of a ruse. The officer of the guard on the gate (I assumed he was an English public school boy) said to me, 'Whither goest thou?'

I answered in what I thought was a convincing imitation of an Oxford accent, '*We* would have said, "*Quo Vadis?*"'

He opened the gate for me, held out his hand and said, 'Vale.' He had heard the sum total of my Latin.

Inside the barracks, I had seen a man dressed in the uniform of the Flying Corps. I had watched this man in town, where he was always dressed in civilian clothes. He was obviously doing some kind of intelligence. I passed the word on to our headquarters.

It seemed obvious to me, from my brief inspection of Beggar's Bush Barracks, that another turn of the screw would

---

60 One of the locations where members of the 'Cairo gang' of British agents were assassinated on Bloody Sunday.

have broken the low morale of the Auxiliaries. Nothing, however, came of my plan to penetrate their headquarters with Volunteers or sympathisers. My own brief visit, I should point out, was comparatively safe. No one in that barracks that day had thought me to be anything other than British. The Auxiliaries and Black and Tans in Ireland were always on their best behaviour with their compatriots, and very careful to conceal their excesses from the English people.

UNTIL THE TRUCE

THROUGHOUT MUCH OF this period, I lived in a house that was exactly opposite Michael Lynch's home, where Mick Collins was very frequently harboured. This was called Walter House, and the terraced house I lived in was number 109 Richmond Road. Behind Richmond Road – in those days – stretched big green fields and open country. Opposite 109 Richmond Road, and beyond Walter House, were the grounds of Croke Park, from which could often be heard – it seemed very close at hand – the vast roar of the crowds at hurling or Gaelic football matches, organised by the nationally celebrated Gaelic Athletic Association. It now seemed to me to be a long time since those earliest GAA events that I had attended in London at Heme Hill, and those other playing fields where I had first met Michael Collins ...

INSIDE THE GPO

From 1919 to 1921, I would say there were always at least a dozen Volunteers living in my house at 109 Richmond Road. And at no time during the whole period were we raided.

Richard Walsh from County Mayo brought many of his Mayo men to the house where I lived. I instructed them in the elements of the use of explosives. My knowledge was rudimentary. It was possible to use or demonstrate the use of explosives only with crude batteries and modest-sized accumulators. Most of the men lacked the necessary technical knowledge to make explosives, and indeed at that period there was no one more competent than I to give instructions. In retrospect, I hate to think of the possible consequences of my ignorance. With the huge quantity of explosive material we often had in the house, we might very easily have blown 109 Richmond Road and the other houses of the handsome Victorian terrace – and also Mick Collins' Walter House opposite – halfway across Croke Park.

Around that time, a raid was made on Lord French's mail in the Rotunda sorting office. Curiously enough, a copy of John Mitchel's Jail Journal was found among his personal papers.

During that period, approximately from late 1920 to February 1921, an 'unofficial' raid was carried out on a post office or a post office savings bank. I do not know the exact place.

Two men carried out this raid. One of them I knew to be in great want. He was unemployed, and did not even have enough to eat. It would have been extremely awkward for our Volunteer GHQ to carry out any form of punishment: the man and his accessory escaped from Ireland later.

But I wish to make it clear that our GHQ endeavoured to restrain such excesses. On one occasion, an officer of the Volunteers, having raided a post office, used some of the proceeds to buy some equipment for his brigade. I know that this officer was in desperate need of such equipment, but he was immediately suspended and, I assume, subsequently court-martialled.

As an illustration of what one might consider fantastic moral discipline throughout the movement, I know for a fact that a Volunteer officer was on one occasion given what was to him a normal duty – to carry out an execution. On being briefed for the task, he was informed of the name of the person to be executed, and he immediately declined to carry out the duty, because he said that the person whom he was ordered to execute had once struck him. He said that if he carried out such a duty, he might have a private animus, and that, to his mind, would constitute murder. This Volunteer's explanation was accepted as being quite rational, and another Volunteer was detailed for that duty.

HARRY WALPOLE INCIDENT

At some time prior to the Mount Street shootings, some attempt to contact the British government was made by a Volunteer called Harry Walpole. I believe that Harry was to some extent influenced by members of the Dublin medical profession, who were appalled by the increasing frequency of ambushes and their effects on civilians, principally on pregnant women. I couldn't help thinking then, and still do, that Harry Walpole's preoccupation with the safety of civilians was analogous to the compassion felt and expressed, and the concerned actions taken as a result, on behalf of the Dublin people, by Pearse and our other leaders in those last days of the Easter Rising.

By this time, during much of 1921, our forces were increasingly on the offensive against the British Auxiliaries and the Black and Tans. This led to extensive large-scale reprisals by the enemy, who very often, having failed to engage us effectively, relieved their fear and frustration by attacks on the civilian population. Those reprisals, carried out against our people in town or country, made the Volunteers even more popular; every atrocity gained us more support. The Volunteers, and the growing Sinn Féin political party, of whom they were the militant arm, were becoming an attractive alternative to the panic and disarray of British law and disorder. The number of ambushes and running battles escalated.

Poorer communities suffered most. As ever, it was the poorer people who hid us and fed us. But the rebels were now gaining active support from the professional and the new middle class; Protestants, nationalist Catholics and even the ascendancy itself – indeed, particularly the ascendancy – began to find us an attractive alternative to a system that was breaking down.

Some high-ranking members of the English cabinet were attempting to make contact with us. Overtures were being made through Harry Walpole's agency and, I believe, through Sir Brian McMahon, and some other doctor whose name I now forget, a bacteriologist who lived, I think, in Earlsfort Terrace – near where the actor and writer Micheál MacLiammóir lives today.

Harry Walpole told me that discussions were held and that full fiscal autonomy for Ireland was mentioned; that a representative of England had come over and had made proposals to Sir Brian McMahon and another doctor; and that a possible plan for settlement could be offered. Harry also told me that he had approached Arthur Griffith and put this proposal before him, and that he had said to Griffith during that conversation: 'But, Mr Griffith, you could be the first President of –' and that Griffith called Walpole 'an impudent pup' and ordered him out of the room.

My purpose in relating this incident is to illustrate that at no time was Harry Walpole threatened, or put under any restraint, by Volunteer GHQ – any more than I had been, after my personal sortie into Beggars Bush Barracks. It was a time of strangely individual initiatives. And, considering that the IRB to a large extent dominated our GHQ, there would appear to have been remarkable forbearance.

TRANSPORT OF ARMS TO DUBLIN

Some time later (in February 1921), Richard Walsh asked me to go with him to London, to buy arms for the Mayo brigades. I told him that I had a limited job to do for the Mid-Limerick Brigade, but that when I had fulfilled this duty, I would go with him and give him all the assistance I could in procurement of arms in England. I told Walsh that it was likely to prove very expensive, and that I personally had no intention of seeking or of handling large sums of money for this purpose.

Our main contact for the procurement of arms in London was Robert Browne – later my brother-in-law. Walsh secured some arms through this source, but, when we came to transport them to Ireland, we encountered some difficulty. The man who was presumed to be an authority on the means of transport by ships was Ned Golding. He told me that the route from London to Dublin by sea was closed, and that if we dispatched these arms, we would do so without his permission.

Jack Sherlock was a bosun on a ship of the Lady Line. He was quite willing to take the arms aboard, stow them away and bring them to Ireland. Living near the London docks was a stevedore named Mahoney, a grandson of an Irishman who'd left Ireland during the famine. He was willing to place such arms aboard boats travelling to Dublin. With the assistance of these two men, and notwithstanding Golding's dissent, Walsh and I succeeded in getting some arms transported to Dublin.

The stevedore, Mahoney, took me on as a dock labourer, and I was thus able to see the possibility of getting arms on to the boats. By securing this job, I had some hope of discovering if it were possible to export larger quantities of arms into Ireland. Huge Jacob's biscuit crates were hoisted aboard the boat, and they were not inspected. I knew this to be so, because I made one journey in one of the Lady boats with Jack Sherlock. En route to Ireland, we touched at four or five ports on the English and Welsh coastlines. We had some arms aboard and, of necessity, had to shift them to various places in the hold of the boat during our journey.

It seemed remarkable to me that Jack Sherlock did this job for a considerable period, perhaps eighteen months, moving small cargoes of arms to different places on the boat. The vessel was inspected at every port and never once, as far as I know, did he lose a weapon.

But at no time was the import of arms through these channels anything but a trickle. I feel I should stress this, because legends abound which allege otherwise.

On the fringe of the revolutionary movement, there was a large contingent of theatrical types – and some theatre people who had, even from the week of the Rising, worked hard and fought staunchly for the movement. Among these was the Abbey Theatre and later Hollywood actor Arthur Shields, Barry Fitzgerald's brother, who was with us in the Post Office during Easter Week. And, of course, there was that other Abbey Theatre actor, the first man to be killed in Easter Week; that is, according to the lines from the W.B. Yeats poem: '... the first man to be shot that day/Was the player, Connolly'[61].

But there was also a more questionable element at work. On one occasion, I was shown a quantity of jewellery, and was informed that there was perhaps twenty or thirty times such a quantity, elsewhere. The sample I was shown filled a Primrose fifty-cigarette box. The person who showed it to me told me that this jewellery had been sent to London from Dublin for disposal. I thought that this was rather fishy, as I knew that one of the people in London was connected with one of the raiding parties at the same time that Lord French's mail was captured. I assumed that this jewellery was captured in that raid.

---

61 No relation to James Connolly, Sean Connolly was the earliest Irish casualty of the men involved in the attack on Dublin Castle on Easter Monday 1916.

I immediately notified Michael Collins. Mick Collins wrote back to me, and told me to inquire into the matter with Sean McGrath, who was at that time a member of the Self-Determination Committee. I didn't take the person who possessed this jewellery to Sean McGrath, but ordered him, on the authority I had received from Michael Collins, to explain his possession of the jewellery to McGrath. I knew this man's brother, and I did not wish to know anything further to the discredit of a comrade. I took no further interest in the matter, but Michael Collins, in his letter, implied that such goods should have been utterly destroyed. I was told – and I believed it to be true – that all this jewellery was subsequently destroyed, on instructions from our GHQ.

There seemed to be some jealousy among some of the men who were associated with the Volunteer movement in London, and I assume that this was the reason we were deterred from using the available boats to transport arms. Edmond Browne and his brother, Bob (to whom I have already referred), were zealous and enterprising, and they had both used their own money for the purchase of guns. They made the most worthwhile contacts for the purchase of other arms. I can assume that hostility to these men arose because of their efficiency, and because they were relative newcomers to the revolutionary movement.

Richard Walsh and I went into a large number of towns in the north of England, seeking arms. We picked them up, one or two at a time. Irish countrymen in England were very friendly to us when they knew our purpose. Richard Walsh carried large sums of money – perhaps four or five hundred pounds – on those trips, and he was never molested, although in Sheffield we at one time rubbed shoulders, of necessity, with a criminal ring. I assume that the fear that the Irishmen aroused, and the obvious respect for Dick Walsh, were the main reasons why Dick walked about in security.

From that period until the Truce in 1921, we did little but pick up a few arms here and there. We were well aware at that time that the active Volunteers in Dublin and Ireland were said to be cutting down .303 cartridges to fit their weapons.

Richard Walsh dispatched a substantial cargo of arms via the Liverpool route. It weighed about two hundredweight. Another cargo he dispatched through the London route, with the help of Jack Sherlock, also reached Dublin. Dick had arranged that this cargo, intended for his lads in Mayo, would be picked up by two ladies, who would arrive at the arms dump in Dublin with a hackney car. But, as the result of a misunderstanding, the person responsible for issuing the arms from the dump failed to keep his appointment – and our GHQ seized Dick's hard-got shipment. I did not consider them lost, because I did not care who in Ireland got final possession of those arms, so long as it was not the enemy.

Later, I delivered my collection to Garret MacAuliffe of Newcastle West. For the original sixty pounds I had been given, I delivered only six weapons – revolvers and automatics, and some ammunition.

When the Truce was declared,[62] I returned to Dublin and went to work, mostly as an electrician again, in Wicklow, Galway and Mayo. For a time it was very peaceful. But the negotiations for the Treaty were advancing and, soon after, Collins and Griffith returned from London to the newly founded Dáil Éireann. Then came the split, and the walk-out of de Valera's party.[63]

I had thought for about two years that the method of appointing our officers would lead to trouble at some future date. A number of men were approved solely because of their popularity and social position. One case I knew of was very peculiar: an officer was appointed mainly because his brother had supposedly fought in the GPO. I knew that the brother had not been in the GPO – but I did have the mortification of attending a ceremony at the alleged hero's grave. I told our brigadier that I knew the man, and his whereabouts during Easter Week – which was a long way from the GPO. He said that he suspected this – but that the man selected had local prestige. In the time to come, the country paid dearly for the granting of those high-sounding commissions. It was one of the causes of the Civil War ...

---

62 11 July 1921.

63 The Treaty was ratified on 7 January 1922, by seven votes, in Dáil Éireann. De Valera and his followers refused to accept it, and withdrew.

EPILOGUE

JOE GOOD'S journal ends there. In this narrative, which he wrote over a period of about a year, whenever he came to thoughts of the Civil War, there was a hiatus in his writing. He would just come to a stop. Each time this occurred, he insisted that he would not – indeed could not – write any further, though he would yield eventually to my persuasion and continue his journal. In this last instance, however, he was immovable. Having reached the beginning of the Civil War in his personal odyssey, he had clearly decided he could write no further.

Joe withdrew from this fight between fellow Irishmen. When the Civil War broke out, he resigned from the army in which he had been commissioned as a lieutenant, and attempted to withdraw from active participation in the movement. But not for long. The death of Michael Collins, in an ambush near his home town of Clonakilty in west

Cork, was a personal tragedy for my father. It brought him back immediately into the Free State army.

In a conflict that had riven the country, it was not surprising that Joe lost some old friendships, but gained others that were to last for life. He was admired and respected by his superiors and comrades, as an efficient, professional officer. The Civil War was brought to a speedy end by the efforts of resilient men such as Joe. Their capacity for daring and initiative had been honed in action in the GPO, against the British secret service, the RIC, the British army and the Black and Tans.

As with other revolutions, when the fighting was all over, plenty of non-combative heroes emerged from their various sanctuaries, but for his part, Joe Good again resigned his commission. He returned to a quiet civilian life soon after the Civil War ended. He had married a London-Irish girl, Mary Ellen Donovan, and together they had four children, a daughter and three sons. As the years passed, he very rarely participated in patriotic celebrations and, when he did attend reunions of old comrades, he would leave his medals at home. As a small boy, I would often seek them out from their forgotten, hidden place, ribbons and metal as pristine as they had been when they first arrived from government departments years before.

As schoolboys in Dublin in the 1930s and '40s, we boys had a certain edge when it came to answering, 'Where was your father in 1916?' I won a lot of sixpences by bringing many a doubting Tom, Dick and Paddy to the 1916 room at the National Museum, and showing them my father in the official group photograph of the survivors of the GPO garrison. My schoolmates were also slow to believe that so many of these men had been born in England, but I could point them out and point to their names at the bottom of the photograph.

Yet, though we learned a great deal about the part of Collins and other major figures in the Irish revolution from our father, it was Joe's comrades who told us stories of his own bravery. My brother Kevin's favourite story is of Joe's encounter with Black and Tans in a small country town. Some four or five Tans barged into a grocery shop in the town, pushed aside the locals, including Joe, and demanded service. One proceeded to fill a bag with eggs from the counter, while another demanded the chickens that were hanging in the window. They made it clear they had no intention of paying. At that, Joe moved in behind the Tans and produced his Luger pistol. 'Mind you don't get a game-cock,' he advised them dryly, and they fled.

Another such story I heard from my brother, John, only a few years ago. It seems that an American general named Prout had been brought in to give the Free State army professional advice. Joe gave the impression of rather disliking Prout, with whom he served for a time. One day Joe was travelling with a company of soldiers, when they were ambushed by the republican 'Irregulars'; the entire column was trapped, and raked with machine-gun and rifle fire. Joe was sitting beside the driver of the leading lorry, who was shot in the head and killed. Joe was wounded, but managed to take cover while the republican firing continued. When the firing stopped, the Irregulars came down on to the road. One began to rob the boots from Joe's feet, thinking him dead, but when he discovered that Joe was still alive, he cocked his weapon to finish him off. Fortunately, the republican commander stepped forward just then: it was Dan Breen, a leading guerrilla fighter in the War of Independence and later a TD in de Valera's Fianna Fáil party. He recognised Joe as a 1916 man, and this was probably what saved his life.

Breen asked Joe, 'Can you drive a lorry out of this?'

Joe replied, 'I could drive a bloody aeroplane out of this!'

Breen then asked Joe to drive one of the lorries to town (my brother does not remember where), to get a priest for the men lying dead on the road. Joe drove back, contacted a priest, and then went straight to the army barracks. He went into the officers' mess, bloody and bootless. Prout and the other officers were at lunch. Haughtily, Prout asked Joe why he was entering the mess 'unsuitably dressed'.

'Well, the column has been ambushed,' Joe answered laconically, 'but don't worry. I've just got them a priest.'

Joe knew many of the Irregulars, his former comrades. In this war of brother against brother, he thought it prudent to arm himself with a revolver strapped to his thigh, and at night he kept the gun under his pillow. In the latter part of the Civil War, he served as OC in that part of County Monaghan which projects into the Six Counties. He and his young wife were sometimes invited to social occasions by the Anglo-Irish gentry in the border area, presumably to encourage the Free State troops to protect their property from arson.

He also served in Kilkenny, and would recount a story about one of his fellow soldiers firing an artillery piece. As the man pulled the lanyard to fire the shell, he shouted at Joe, 'Jaysus, Joe, this is the sport of kings!' There is a chilling reminder in that tale of the fighting witnessed in our own time in the Balkans.

Joseph Good put these experiences behind him. He settled with his family in the then rural village of Templeogue. The unpolluted River Dodder ran by, curving its way towards Ringsend and Joyce's Anna Livia Plurabelle, the River Liffey, whose quays were crowded with pubs and bookstalls. Templeogue was five miles from the centre of the city, and each day he cycled there to work. Then a second World War engulfed Europe. We followed the progress of armies on a map hung on the kitchen wall, and on the wireless we heard of the fall and dismemberment of nations, of Auschwitz and Buchenwald and the first atom bombs. History had assumed the face of apocalypse.

INSIDE THE GPO

Joe Good became a gardener; our small house in Temple-ogue was embowered in roses. Starved for flowers as a child, he acquired a hundred rose bushes, and was later to exceed that number. Loganberries and raspberries, apple and plum trees vied for space with onions, celery, radishes and leeks. Under Joe's domestic generalship, we grew all of our own vegetables on county allotments, and cut and harvested the family fuel on the turf-banks of the Dublin Mountains. The 'little' revolution of his past seemed diminished. Joe was little more than a boy in 1916, and a youth — if a mature one — during the earliest of the Irish 'Troubles'.

My father's reluctance to be drawn into patriotic events increased with the years; his anti-heroic posture became his trademark. Because he did not attend national celebrations, old comrades had to come to him. Frequent callers included Joe Leonard, Paddy Daly, Garret MacAuliffe, or Johnny 'Blimey' O'Connor, who had fought on the republican side in the Civil War.

Our family harvested the Dublin Mountains, bring-ing home bushels of blackberries, mushrooms, walnuts and hazelnuts in autumn, to keep the larder full. Relatives, neigh-bours and casual passers-by bore away the surplus: armfuls of food and flowers from Joe's cornucopia. All holidays, Christ-mas especially, were indulgent festivals — a far cry from the want and scarcity of his London childhood. Joe was a worker, a self-sufficient provider from before the age of ten, driven by a Protestant ethic that made him something of an eccentric among people who survived on laissez-faire.

He assumed the character of a myth, a fighter against local injustices. He was feared by bullies twice his size. He could be a fearsome opponent. Men respected him, and women liked him.

He never mellowed. He never lost his distaste for narrow chauvinism. He was a moderate socialist. He was physically awkward, and lacked social poise. He sang a little off-key, but we never told him that he did so. He had intellect, venerated learning and talent of any kind, and remained always curious, tolerant, questing and open-minded. Some said he lacked a sense of humour, but he had humour in an almost Elizabethan sense. It was urbane and ironic, like his accent, which was Churchillian, but with an Irish cadence. His accent was his own invention.

It was a voice that had something in common with that of the greatest romantic 'Irish' actor, the late Mícheál MacLiammóir. Both remained English in discipline, taste and character, but had won the right to call themselves Irish. Both invented their voices and, to some extent, invented themselves. One invented a name and helped to give a new country a theatre. The other helped to invent that country, to bring it into being.

Joe Good was a hard man to know, and though he was a hard man to love, he was greatly loved by many. After my mother's death, Joe married the poet Pamela Heal, granddaughter of the Irish poet John Todhunter. But Pamela was not to enjoy his company for long. He died at the age of sixty-seven, after surviving multiple heart attacks brought on by the emphysema caused by smoking strong, cheap cigarettes for fifty years. To the end, he proved a hard man to kill.

On his death in 1962, his son Kevin, his only child then living in Dublin, requested that the funeral be private, and that there be no flowers. This wish was respected; the house and the chapel afterwards were attended only by immediate family and intimate friends. His old comrade, Johnny O'Connor, on holiday in the south of Ireland, heard his death lamented in the mountains of County Kerry, and immediately drove non-stop to Dublin to arrange a full military funeral. A single rose was carried by his widow to be left on the coffin. When the hearse left the church, it was followed by a half-mile-long procession of cars occupied by friends.

When the cortège neared the country graveyard, at the feet of the Dublin Mountains at Bothar-na-Breena, the hillside was covered with people. We stopped the cortège a few hundred yards from the gates, and Paddy Carmody, a young admirer, added his shoulder to those of Joe's three sons. We carried the coffin through heavy rain to the waiting priest and the honour-guard of the Irish army, a smart squad, drenched, alert, their young eyes in very young faces looking intensely clear beside rifles held at attention.

The crowd gathered closer; the tricolour, folded by the officer of the guard, was handed to the family; the single rose was placed and the coffin lowered; the rifles were raised and the saluting volleys fired. We kept the flag. We buried his three medals with him: their bright ribbons and bronze were his, well earned; a part of his journey, not ours.

I had asked Mrs Georgiana Yeats, the widow of our national poet, for permission to have a few words of Yeats' inscribed on my father's gravestone. Despite the fact that my father had quoted Yeats to us all of his life, he would have been intrigued and surprised at the idea of an obscure ex-revolutionary being accorded an honour in a manner so close in style to that which our greatest poet had arranged for himself. I was moved by Mrs Yeats' letter, agreeing to our request: 'Weren't we all stirred in the same pot?' she said. The words on Joe's gravestone are from 'The Circus Animals' Desertion':

... and yet when all is said

It was the dream itself enchanted me.

Maurice Good, Dublin, 1996

16LIVES

The Easter Rising of 1916 was an attempt by armed
revolutionaries to overthrow British rule in Ireland.
A small group of Irishmen and Irishwomen seized key
buildings in Dublin and fought a pitched battle with British
soldiers for one week. The execution of sixteen men
awakened a generation to the cause of Irish freedom.

16 Lives will record the full story of those executed leaders …

16 LIVES

John O'Callaghan

16 LIVES EAMONN CEANNT

Mary Gallagher

16 LIVES EDWARD DALY

Helen Litton

16 LIVES JAMES CONNOLLY

Lorcan Collins

16 LIVES

Honor Ó Brolcháin

16 LIVES MICHAEL MALLIN

Brian Hughes

16 LIVES ROGER CASEMENT

Angus Mitchell

16 LIVES SEÁN HEUSTON

John Gibney

16 LIVES SEÁN MACDIARMADA

Brian Feeney

16 LIVES THOMAS CLARKE

Helen Litton

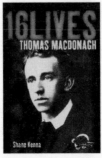

16 LIVES THOMAS MACDONAGH

Shane Kenna

16 LIVES

Katherine Sheppard